BULL FEVER

Chase brave employment with a naked sword
Throughout the world.

GEORGE HERBERT

BULL
FEVER

by KENNETH TYNAN

HARPER & BROTHERS, NEW YORK

TO ELAINE

Contents

Illustrations

9

Preface

By profession, I am a drama critic; by conviction, a believer in the abolition of capital punishment; by birth, English. The reader may find it odd that a lover of the mimic deaths of stage tragedy, an enemy of judicial killing, and a native of a country which has immemorially detested those blood sports which involve personal hazard should have succumbed to bull fever, joined the *afición*, become a friend and apologist of the Spanish bullfight. And indeed it *is* odd. Or so I thought for many weeks after I saw my first *corrida* in 1950. But now the bullfight seems to me a logical extension of all the impulses my temperament holds—love of grace and valor, of poise and pride; and, beyond these, the capacity to be exhilarated by mastery of technique. No public spectacle in the world is more technical, offers less to the untaught observer, than a bullfight.

C. M. Bowra defines the task of the epic hero as "the pursuit of honour through risk." The clearest modern encapsulation of that pursuit is in bullfighting: for though honor is riskly pursued by pilots and mountaineers, their sphere of action is remote from most of us. The bullfighter brings the pursuit down to earth and reduces it to a pattern. The connection with tragedy, as some novelists seem almost obscenely aware, is even closer, though I did not realize how close until a few months ago, when I found confirmation in—of all places—Charlotte Brontë. I was rereading the mar-

13

velous chapter of *Villette* in which she recreates the acting of
Rachel, who is lightly disguised under the name of Vashti. I was
agog, as ever, with envy of the fine, precise, vividly moving cadences
—"a queen, fair as the day once, turned pale now like twilight, and
wasted like wax in flame"—and then I paused, arrested by the pas-
sage in which the authoress tries to sum up the impact of the ap-
parently irreconcilable qualities which went to the making of
Vashti's sorcery:

> It was a marvellous sight; a mighty revelation.
> It was a spectacle low, horrible, immoral.
> Swordsmen thrust through, and dying in their blood on the arena
> sand; bulls goring horses disembowelled, made a meeker vision for the
> public—a milder condiment for a people's palate—than Vashti, torn
> by seven devils . . .

Now Charlotte Brontë had never seen a bullfight in her life. But
I know exactly what she meant; it was a right instinct that made
her seek a similitude where she did. Other plays and other actors
evoke, for me, the same response; especially *Othello*, a dramatized
bullfight if ever there was one, with its hero the courageously blundering bull, lured to his death by the matador Iago and that maddening handkerchief. Henry Irving was aware of the parallel. He said
that he found in Iago "a slight dash of the bullfighter," and that
during the fight between Cassio and Montano he used "to enjoy a
mischievous sense of mastery by flicking at them with a red cloak, as
if they were bulls in the arena." The jealousy scene (III, iii), which
is the heart of the most perfectly constructed play Shakespeare
wrote, could be regarded as a matador's literary vade-mecum: it has
every pass in the book.

To explore these hints, to explain the kind of pleasure the bullfight can bestow, I have written this book. It is an acount of a dozen

bullfights, seen within the space of three weeks in various towns and cities on the Iberian peninsula. I do not claim that it is anything like a definitive survey of modern tauromachy: I have seen fewer than eighty *corridas* in my life. It simply covers the bulls and the fighters, the styles and the rivalries, as they were in the summer of 1952; and the experiences, alternately vile and glorious, which I had in their presence.

London, 1954   K. T.

BULL FEVER

1

The Shape of the Fight

To BEGIN with, a glance at the hard words and the sequence of a Spanish bullfight.

1. *The whole:* is known as *la lidia*, the game. It is a *corrida de toros* if the bulls are to be killed by matadors, bullfighters who have graduated beyond the apprentice stage of their careers. In this case the bulls must be not less than four or more than seven years old. It is a *novillada* if the fighters are *novilleros*, apprentice killers; in which case the bulls must not be less than three years old. In either case each bull will be *bos taurus ibericus*, a wild animal as different from the agricultural variety as an armored car is from a haywain. The fight is held in a *plaza de toros*, or bullring, to which each fighter will bring his squadron (*cuadrilla*) of assistants, usually consisting of three *banderilleros* and two *picadores*. The gray-faced man peering over the *barrera*, the plank fence which separates the *toreros* from the bulls, is the fighter's *apoderado* or agent.

2. *The parts:* (a) First trumpet. The ceremonial march, or *paseo*, of the *toreros* across the arena (Plates 3 and 4). *Torero* means anyone, mounted or dismounted, who makes a living out of fighting bulls. The word *toreador*, popularized by Bizet, is an archaism meaning a mounted bullfighter.

(b) Second trumpet. The entrance of the bull through the *toril* gate. Capework ensues, passes made with the *capote* or *capa*, the yellow-and-magenta fighting cape. It is used first by the senior matador's squadron, so that he can observe the bull's demeanor and qualities, and then by the matador himself.These passes may include the *verónica* (Plates 12 and 13), the *media-verónica* (Plate 14), the *larga cambiada* (Plate 15), the *gaonera*, named after its inventor, Rodolfo Gaona (Plate 16), and the *chicuelina*, named after Chicuelo (Plate 17).

(c) Third trumpet. The entrance of the picadors, mounted on blindfold horses and carrying their picks, spiked punishing poles eight feet six inches in length. An iron guard near the tip prevents more than four inches' penetration into the bull's flesh. Each horse is strapped into a *peto*, a thick mattress which protects its chest, legs, stomach and hindquarters. When the bull charges the horse, the picador leans over and inserts the pick into its shoulders, the aim being to weaken its tossing muscle (*morrillo*) and to test its courage and resistance (Plate 19). The *suerte de varas*, or trial of the picks, ends when the bullring president decides—normally after three or four picks have jabbed in and out. Between picks, the bull is lured away from the horse in a *quite*, or rescue, performed by the matadors in order of seniority. In each quite the fighter is expected to repeat part of his repertoire with the cape.

To employ Ernest Hemingway's terminology, this is the bull's trial.

(d) Fourth trumpet. Banderillas—thick wooden sticks twenty-eight inches long, decorated with frills of colored paper and ending in a steel harpoon point—are placed in pairs into the bull's withers, either by the matador himself or (more usually) by his *banderilleros* or *peónes*. Up to four pairs may be put in. If the bull is a coward (*toro manso*), the president may signal for the use of black banderillas, which have an arrowhead tip for extra punishment. The banderilleros generally put the sticks in *al cuarteo* (Plate 22), running toward the bull in a quarter circle and popping them over the horns; rarer methods (*al quiebro*, for example) are left to the matador (Plate 23). The object is to tire the bull and lower its head so that the matador can work close to it.

This is the bull's sentencing.

(e) Fifth trumpet. The matador now removes his black winged hat (*montera*) and dedicates the death of the bull either to the president, to a selected spectator, or to the crowd as a whole. When the dedication (*brindis*) is over, he begins his *faena*—the solo series of passes he must perform with the *muleta*, a piece of heavy crimson serge draped over a stick, and the *estoque* or *espada*, the killing sword.

The faena frequently begins with a few low, chopping passes (Plate 25) to test the bull's alertness and endurance; but the basic, classic pass is the *natural*, in which the muleta, held in either the right or the left hand, is swung across the body, taking the bull with it. The sword never leaves the right hand. When it is pricked into the muleta, the area of cloth presented as the bull's target is enlarged, and the pass is less dangerous to make; accordingly a left-hand natural (Plates 29, 30 and 33) is more highly regarded than a right-hand one (Plates 40, 41 and 42). Any pass with the right hand is a *derechazo*. Other passes may include: the *pase de pecho* (chest pass), always used to complete a series of naturals (Plate 26); the *molinete* (Plate 31 shows the kneeling version), *afarolado* (Plate 36), *manoletina* (Plate 35), *arrucina* (Plate 37), *ayudado por alto* or *estatuario* (statuary pass—Plates 27 and 28), and many more. Between passes, occasional *adornos* or *desplantes* (Plates 38, 39 and 43) are permissible—show-off tricks, in which the matador may kneel with his back to the bull, stroke the horn, bite it, or even (as the Mexican Carlos Arruza used to do) rest elbow and chin on the bull's head, as if telephoning (*el teléfono*).

The kill itself may be delivered *a volapié* (with flying feet, i.e., charging the bull) or *recibiendo* (receiving, i.e., awaiting the bull's charge). The latter method, which is immensely hard to perform beautifully, has almost died out. The volapié is executed with the man about ten feet from the bull, the sword in his right hand and the muleta in his left. He attacks, keeping the bull's eye focused on the muleta, swung low and across his body (Plates 44, 45 and 46), and pushes the sword in high over the horns between the shoulder blades. A sword thrust which hits bone or for any reason fails to penetrate is a *pinchazo*; one which goes halfway up to the hilt is a *media-estocada*; one which goes all the way in is an *estocada* (Plate 48). If the bull is still not dead, the matador may choose the *descabello*, taking a sword with a cross piece a few inches from the point, which he stabs down at the bull's neck, severing the spinal cord and felling the animal like a tree (Plate 50).

This is the bull's execution. It is then dragged out to the knackers' yard by a team of gaily beribboned horses or mules.

If the matador's work has been brave and artistic, the president may decide to award him a trophy, sliced from the bull he has killed —an ear (*oreja*); two ears; two ears and the tail (*rabo*); or two ears, the tail, and a hoof (*pata*). Tails and hoofs are not awarded in Madrid, where they are thought vulgar.

The whole bull killing has taken about twenty minutes—five for the picks, five for the banderillas, and ten for the faena. The divisions are known as the thirds (*tercios*) of the fight. In a normal corrida of six bulls, the process will be repeated six times, each of the three matadors taking two bulls. If there are eight bulls, there will be four matadors. If only two men are engaged, the fight is a *mano a mano*, or hand-to-hand. The bulls will have come to the ring from an accredited *ganadería*, or breeding farm. The pastime in which they are the leading figures is the *fiesta brava*, the valiant festival. Its followers are *aficionados*.

We shall drop italics now, except when introducing new words.

2

Pamplona

THE best way to Pamplona, which lies in the foothills of the Spanish Pyrenees, is the lazy way, through Biarritz, St. Jean de Luz, and San Sebastian. The time to go is July, and the right mood one of riot. Sated with shellfish, I plunged inland from San Sebastian's bright half-moon beach and when, late on a Saturday evening, I arrived at Pamplona, the great Fair of San Fermín had already begun, the signal to erupt had been given, with a noontide rocket from the Town Hall, and the panic was on. The annual orgy, an ordeal by noise and wine, the explosion of an under-entertained race, was in spate and many deafening whims were being widely indulged. The town sounded as hell might sound if the people there laughed instead of weeping. The streets were full of dancing men, wearing the prescribed costume of white shirt, white trousers, red cummerbund, and red neckerchief, and there was a whiff of venery in the air. There always is in Spain: a flavor of the violent past, a flavor of hunting, for the Spanish will hunt anything, boar or bull or eagle, relishing the skill and the risk of it. In their view of death there is a traditional stoicism, which is replaced, when the fiesta breaks, with an equally traditional defiance.

A little scared, we dined at a club just outside the town, and found the members shooting live pigeons. I ordered *arroz a la Valenciana*, rice in the Valencian style, and watched for a while the flutter of bloody gray wings and the savage wringing of necks. "Pigeons on the grass," I said, rather wanly, "alas."

My wife finished a mouthful of rice. "Arroz," she said philosophically, "is arroz is arroz."

A burly, dangerous-looking woman in horn-rimmed spectacles picked up a rifle and motioned to the trap boys to release a pigeon. As it rose, flapping to become airborne, she fired, hitting the tip of its right wing; for a moment it lost height, and then flew up and away. We watched it circling the dim amphitheater of hills across the valley, and then returning to base, where a boy caught it and replaced it in one of the shiny green boxes on the terrace. These were homing pigeons. We went afterward to the fairground, spending a long time at a booth which offered an array of cheap plates and cups, and eight wooden balls for a peseta with which to smash them. No prizes were offered, but we were satisfied; we both felt closer to the spirit of this loony fair.

Pamplona, more than any other Spanish town, is bull-crazy and bull-happy; and it is no crude village, but a graciously planned and slumless city. It stands on a plateau overlooking the River Arga, where it was built as the home of the Kings of Navarre, whose domain was annexed in 1512 by Ferdinand of Castile; its arrow-straight avenues debouch, in every direction, upon vistas of smoke-blue hills and what the local guidebook calls "smooth and odoriferous fields." "You would never think," it goes on, "about the different landscapes in such short distances." This regal and cleanly place has a unique distinction. Only Pamplona may announce and hold, every morning of the feria at 7 A.M., an encierro or "enclosing" of bulls. From the corrals at the rim of the town to the tree-girt bullring at the center, each day's bulls are run through the streets. Later, between 5:30 and 8 P.M., they will be ceremoniously and more or less attractively killed.

I rose at six next morning to watch the running, expecting to find no more than a few late rakehells in the slate-gray streets. I was, if anything, too late: thousands of red-eyed wine squirters were there ahead of me, prancing in their sandals, chanting the endless songs of the district. They embraced me and, divining that I was English, spoke to me in hysterical French; one of them, yesterday's railway porter but now a man of holiday, gripped me by the lapels, fixed me with gloomy eyes, and sang, in the tones of one engrossed in worship: "Ease a long way to Tipperary, ease a long way to go. . . ." He returned to me about ten minutes later looking distraught, as if he had forgotten a vital message, and led me into a shop doorway. Here he pinioned me and: "Ease a long way," he said, very furtively and rhythmically, "Ease a *long* way to Tipperary."

Then, in a distance, a rocket banged, meaning that eight black bulls had plunged out of the corral and, escorted by a quartet of belled steers, were headed our way. The crowd cried out, frightened but much moved. Now we could hear the bulls, moving fast and clattering on the cobbles. The mob in the street thinned a little, many of them vaulting over the plank fences which keep the bulls on course, but a majority remained, sharing an ambition: to run alongside a bull, with one hand touching its tossing muscle, which is held to be a well-spring of perpetual courage. The runners were reaching a frantic speed, when: "Look!"—I heard the yell all round me—"Look who is there! The professor!" And there, clad like the rest, he was indeed: the tall, slim-faced maestro himself, the number one matador of Spain since Manolete's death, Luis Miguel González, nicknamed Dominguín. "Hey Luis!" The applause was terrific as he ran past, a hundred yards ahead of the bulls, two of which he was contracted to kill that afternoon. Seven bulls went by, and there was a moment's lull before the spectators in the highest bal-

conies shouted the warning: *"Toro solo!"* The eighth bull, outrun
by the others, comes round the corner on its own, chopping and
hooking, nastily bewildered. A fighting bull being the only animal
which will attack a human being on sight, there is great danger.
It cuts into the crowd, which has relaxed too soon, and now falls
over itself to escape, jabs with the right horn, jabs again, and
romps off. No one has been killed, but a man is gripping his inner
thigh, looking very strained, and bleeding through his trousers.
This is nothing, the ex-porter tells me: five years ago an Urquijo
bull killed two boys and sent two more to hospital. This is nothing
at all.

In the bullring about fifteen thousand people sit fanning themselves, awaiting the runners and the bulls. A lone scout is first in,
half a mile ahead of the others, but he makes a great production of
his entrance, pointing over his shoulders and miming frightful
disasters, like the messenger in a tragedy. First a trickle, then a
full, tumbling flood of boys pursue him; no women, because this
is a masculine prerogative; and at last, out of the dark streets into
the white light of the ring, the bulls come jogging and bumping,
trampling the fallen, who curl up and feign death. A wide-lunged
roar goes up as they cross the arena, guided by the steers to the
shadier corrals behind the stands, where they will remain, standing
ominously under the trees, until the fight.

The ring now fills with those whom fear forbade to tangle with the
big bulls; they leap over the barrier and gather, in attitudes of supplication, beneath the president's box, begging him to release a
young cow to test them. The toril gate is swung back and the
animal catapults into their midst. Its horns are leather padded, but
it can still break ribs with them; the boys scatter like leaves before
the wind, except for those at the perimeter, who stand nobly still,

as toreros should, brandishing old tablecloths and torn newspapers, performing resplendent passes with an adversary thirty yards away. All of them are ready with the expected gesture, the pose of domin-ion. There were no deaths, but a plethora of cuts and bruises, before the cow was taken out, and many left the ring stunned and in-senate.

By seven-thirty it was over. I walked into a town already fully awake and cutting loose. "Be sure," the guidebook said, "you will be our inconditional guests." Although most of the uproar is sheer, innocuous joy, Pamplona has "some most suggestive touristic ways" and in a few of the narrower ones you may lose your passport and pocketbook. "On the contrary," the book inscrutably adds, "the city is gai." Of that there is no doubt at all. Eight untiring bands, bearing banners which advertise cognac and sherry, march the streets day and night, frequently colliding at crossroads, and sur-rounded always, Pied Piper fashion, by the dancers. Tiny boys, dancing they know not why, and old men, dancing they know not how—"merry people," says the book, "amusing themselves and rejoicing the happy visitors." I met and was rejoiced by the man who can roll a cigarette while balancing a glass of anís on his fore-head; and the erudite shoeblack in the flag-hung square, who loves books and music and asked me whether I admired Jawvack. He sang theme after theme, unnecessarily nailing new soles to my shoes, until I recognized Dvorak's New World and shook his hand.

The mendicant game has far fewer exponents in the north of Spain than in the south. In the torrid air of the southern fiestas, at Málaga or Valencia, where the beggars are as numerous as the Cadillacs, the old problem of "Spain, land of contrasts" springs out at you; here in Pamplona it seemed not to exist. So I was musing when a portly child strode out (I think) from under a table at the Café

Kutz, pulled at my coat, and silently extended his hand. Sternly, as other men might demand their birthright, he demanded a cigarette. He looked about six years old. I gave him one. He scrutinized the maker's name, nodded qualified approval, and whipped out from what must have been his armpit a telescopic cigarette holder, nearly a foot long. Wasting no time, he begged a match and lit up.

We fell monosyllabically into conversation. Was I an aficionado? I said I was. Ah, then, he knew a man—his father, as it happened —who could sell me something of immense value. It was a painting. When I said I would like to see it, he strode off, puffing steadily and motioning to me to stay where I was. He returned with a rolled-up canvas under his arm, and what I saw when he unfolded it was immense indeed. It depicted a bullring under a heavy, leaden sky; a great gray bull had just tossed a picador from his horse. But the goring had been averted, for the clouds had parted, and there, descending on a bizarrely tilted cross and holding a fighting cape in one hand, was Christ in person, glowing with an orange incandescence. The bull was turning from the fallen horseman, responding to the quite. The caption read, modestly enough, "A Timely Intervention"; and a stylishly performed one, too, as far as I could judge. The boy told me that the miracle had occurred just over a century ago in a provincial ring; he wanted a thousand pesetas for the picture, which was excessive. When I told him so, he made no attempt to haggle, but simply smiled pityingly at my poverty and made off to the next café. Duveen himself could not have administered a snub with less effort.

For some reason the boy's picture made me think of the hill called Tibidabo, on the outskirts of Barcelona, whose summit is occupied by two things, jostling side by side—a Basilica of the Sacred Heart and a funfair. If Spain is a paradox, this is one of the clues to it, that the juxtaposition of holy and secular, timeless and temporal, does not strike its people as odd or unnatural. They are sophisticated enough to live on permanent nodding terms with eternity, of which they speak as casually as we speak of tomorrow. More Spaniards turn up for lunch a year late than any other nationality.

The fiesta at Pamplona is linked with the town's patron saint, San Fermín of blessed memory, but there was a fiesta before there was a saint to bless it. The bullfights are more recent still—professional bullfighting is little more than two hundred years old—but the bulls have become the unquestioned heroes of the feast. Everyone in the town is touched and infected with their mystery. You will see priests down at the corrals every morning, peering intently at the bulls; it is hard to conceive of a Protestant clergyman at a corrida. I watched two priests in the square demonstrating to a group of Vassar girls the correct use of the cape and banderillas they had bought as souvenirs: the magenta folds swung softly, while the father pivoted, following with his eyes the trajectory of his imagined bull. It was a priest, too, whose eyes shone as he told me of the two rival Mexican matadors he once saw in San Sebastian: how one, at the climax of the fight, threw away his sword and muleta, and passed the bull with his pocket handkerchief; and how the other outdid him, to screams of alarm, by picking up a handful of sand from the arena, and taking the bull twice past him with grain after grain of it, dropped before its muzzle.

There is no boredom in the ten vacant hours between the encierro and the bullfight: they are spent in a cumulative working-up to fresh frenzy. The luckier dancers, those within earshot of the bands, jig to the tinny complaint of the *gaitas*, woodwinds which sound like bagpipes. The rest seize balloons and pluck at them, producing a tuba-like, grunting noise, just passable as a rhythmic accompaniment to dancing. Tourists can, of course, fill in time by observing the unfailing drollery of other tourists. At the local Turismo office I saw a deaf, middle-aged English traveler, with a sweet-sucking child at his elbow, attempting to explain to the clerk that he wanted to hire a car. The clerk spoke perfect English and understood at once; the Englishman, insulated by his affliction, refused to acknowledge the fact. "See here," he said several times, "I want a car. I *desire* a car. Au-to-mo-bile. Honk, honk." He made steering motions with both hands, narrowing his eyes to keep out the dust. The clerk, who had long since booked the vehicle, smiled politely at this piece of mime. "Car to *hire*," the Englishman went on. "For money. Dinero. Pesetas." He produced a handful of notes and, to the clerk's increasing mystification, rustled them under his nose.

"I have booked a car," the clerk said, slowly and carefully.

"Car!" cried the Englishman. "Now we're getting somewhere. Give the man a sweet, Roland. A car is what I *desire* . . . ."

The English, in general, come to Spain looking as if at any moment it were going to offend them; the Americans, in general, as if they were going to offend it. Ever since Hemingway wrote *The Sun Also Rises*, Pamplona has been a magnet for American left bankers. At the Café Chóko I met one such group, a conclave of expatriates from Pittsburgh, who were camping by the river and wore the black smocks of Basque peasants. One was grim and vexed, having discovered that his mistress was not only a Hungarian countess but also a pyromaniac, but the others were rapidly getting the spirit, drinking fiercely, eating nothing but berries, and singing incessantly. Through whatever tumult in the streets, their voices, whisky-hoarse and somehow unshaven, would faintly filter, chanting the old radio hymn about the good points of Little Orphan Annie:

Who's that little chatterbox,
The one with all the auburn locks,
Who can it be?
It's little Orphan Annie. . . .

"Look, friend, don't give me a hard time," one of them broke off
in argument, "I never slept through a corrida in my life. I'm no
goddamn bulldozer."

Most visitors who are unable to sleep in the afternoon succumb
to the guidebook, which gives details not only of "the pricking
programme of sensational spectacles" offered by the feria, but also
of the surrounding countryside. Roncesvalles is close by, where
Charlemagne came to grief, "a happening of 1st grade in the me-
diaeval Europe"; a little farther off, at Viana, there is a statue of
Cesare Borgia, "the queer knight-errant," killed fighting in the
neighborhood. Myself, I was more attracted by the curiosities of
Pamplona itself, which "conserves the old relish of a fortress." I
visited the palace of the Kings of Navarre, where there is a superb
and jealously guarded Goya: the Marqués de San Adrián, coarsely
elegant, twitching a riding crop, with a look of blue-chinned
désinvolture in which Tony Lumpkin and L'Aiglon unexpectedly
coalesce. I looked, too, at the portraits of the kings themselves,
bulbous and flaccid, and their plain, inordinate doxies. When I
came out into the heat, other kings and queens, garishly daubed
and twenty feet high, were revolving gravely in the streets, attended
by bands of men in big-head masks, who playfully thrashed the
passers-by with inflated bladders. These cretinous masks are taken
out of storage, dusted and worn every year, but nobody seems to
tire of them: novelty, to the Spanish, is not an obligatory virtue.
A little breeze lifted the skirts of the queens and rattled the royal
regalia. I went back to the hotel and dozed nervously. Soon it was
five o'clock, time for the town to converge on the bullring.

1. In the streets, escorted by two black and white steers

2. In the corrals

Cartier-Bresson

Peter Buckley

BULLS IN PAMPLONA

3. Pamplona

THE PARADE

4. Valencia

Peter Buckley

5. Noon. The Apartado: the afternoon's bulls are paired off and their numbers written on scraps of paper, which are then drawn from a hat. Whiteshirted, in the foreground, is Ernest Hemingway

6. Luis Miguel Dominguín and his ex-matador father

Luis Vidal

7. Antonio Ordóñez

Nisberg

8. Miguel Báez, 'Litri'

Cartier-Bresson

9. The expensive seats

10. The cheap seats

11. The protagonist

12. Veronica to the right by Manolo Vázquez

13. Veronica to the left by Manolo Vázquez

Luis Vidal

14. Half-veronica by Manolo Vázquez

15. The large cambiada of Luis Miguel Dominguín

Luis Vidal

16. A gaonera by Litri

Luis Vidal

17. Manolo González in a chicuelina

Luis Vidal

To anyone who believes in hierarchies, the bullfight needs no explanation. The inferior must be ruled by the superior, the superior must rule the inferior; it is a duty imposed by heaven, and because of it the man must rule the bull. Those who invented the Spanish bullfight were unfortunately not philosophers; they were hunters and sportsmen. Wherever there have been fighting bulls they have been hunted: forty centuries ago in Crete, afterward in Greece, and then, according to Pliny, in Julius Caesar's Rome. Nobody is certain who taught the Spanish to adopt the sport, whether it came over with Roman legionaries, or arrived with the Moorish invasions of the seventh century. Surviving accounts, however, make it clear that at the beginning of the Middle Ages bulls were being fought in Spain, and fought in two very dissimilar ways: on the one hand, there existed a savage, lawless, peasant pastime, in which wild bulls were hacked to death, and on the other, a more graceful equestrian sport favored by the nobility. By the end of the thirteenth century, bullfights organized by sporting noblemen were being held to celebrate days of festival; it was an official and aristocratic game, always practiced on horseback, in the manner of modern *rejoneadores* or mounted bullfighters, who are occasionally engaged to kill one bull before the corrida proper, and of whom the most highly skilled is Angel Peralta. Bullfighting on horseback, using a razor-edged lance or *rejon*, reached its climax of popularity during the seventeenth century. That it lost its universal appeal was due to the qualms of Philip V, who made it clear to his court that he had no taste for the barbarities of bull killing; he wanted an aristocracy as civilized as that of Louis XIV in France, and it is as well that he did, because mounted bullfighting, an adroit but unemotional display of horsemanship, at once began to give place to the sterner, more beautiful business of bullfighting on foot. The pedestrian toreros,

hitherto the humble assistants of the riders, now became the principal figures of the spectacle; the professionals ousted the amateurs
forever. Around 1700 there was born in Ronda Francisco Romero,
the first great matador, inventor of the muleta and of the kill
recibiendo, and founder of a dynasty of bullfighters whose names
crowd the early chronicles of modern tauromachy. Bullfighting
literally found its feet in 1724, the year of Romero's first triumphs;
and when, in 1749, the first permanent arena of stone began to be
erected, the bullfight was already acquiring the shape in which
present-day aficionados know it. There were, of course, great differences then. The matador's only task was to kill the bull cleanly and
quickly, and he used the muleta simply to square it into position
with a chop here and a flourish there; few matadors before the
First World War employed more than a dozen passes with the
cloth before going in with the sword. The modern faena de muleta,
nowadays the focus of the bullfight, was the creation of Juan
Belmonte, whose revolutionary career as a matador began when he
took the *alternativa* in Madrid on October 16, 1914. Belmonte, a
grim, dwarfish Sevillian, was born in 1892, retired in 1935, and is
still miraculously alive, having created and practiced a system of
bullfighting which depended on grace, emotion, languor and close-
ness to the horns, and which only Manolete was able to intensify.
Belmonte made bullfighting more exhaustively arduous, more con-
stantly risky, than it had ever been; and it is not to be wondered
at that a matador's career, which before him might have lasted a
quarter of a century, nowadays rarely exceeds ten years. Manolo
González, who fought his first novillada in 1946 and retired rich in
1952, is a fair example. The four matadors contracted to appear at
the first fight in Pamplona were his contemporaries and competitors.

I do not know why they do it, except for the reason that the money is good; but I knew, thirty bullfights before, why I liked watching them. It was because their job is not only hard to do well but hard to do at all. George Moore once pointed out that "ability is required to compose even a bad opera, a bad epic, a bad picture —but anyone can play Juliet and Hamlet badly." There are only a few hundred people in the world who can fight bulls badly; of whom about three dozen are capable of fighting bulls as they should be fought. Once, perhaps, in six attempts, the members of this smaller group will provide an afternoon of appropriate beauty. These triumphs are rare because of the disconcerting way in which the conditions of the bullfight combine to make failure the likeliest outcome. The corrida is a synthesis of the classical and romantic principles which underlie all art and most entertainment, and between which the most delicate balance must be kept if the spectacle is to succeed. It has the lucid formality of classicism, where the whole dominates the parts, plus the violent personal expressiveness of romanticism, where the parts dominate the whole. Good fights are a sort of stalemate; bad ones occur when the personality of the fighter emerges so abundantly that the shape of the afternoon is distorted, or when a fighter's hankering for personal safety impels him to submerge himself in the pattern, in which case he will go perfunctorily through the motions of preparing his bulls with little sincerity and less effect. The first fight at Pamplona was a pretty bad one on both counts.

Of course, it need not have been; all the auspices prophesied the opposite. The day was clear blue and gold. The bulls came from the pastures of a local breeder, Martínez Elizondo of Tudela, who would feel in honor bound to do his best for Pamplona. Their

average weight, as it turned out, was higher than that of any of the
subsequent fights: 625 pounds en canal, which means the dead
weight after the bull has been stripped, skinned, and drained of
blood in the bullring slaughterhouse, and which would be equiva-
lent to about 990 pounds live weight. Bulls fought in first-category
bullrings must have a live weight of not less than 930 pounds; in
second-category rings, of which Pamplona is one, not less than 880
pounds. As far as ponderable considerations went, the Elizondo bulls
looked good. So did the cartel, or program of matadors. The senior,
who would march into the arena on the extreme left of the quartet,
was Luis Miguel Dominguín, the tall, soft-featured, supremely
egotistical Castilian, who was, from the death of Manolete in 1947
up to his own retirement in 1953, the self-confessed *Número Uno*
of living matadors. In 1952 he was twenty-five years old, and
possessed a repertoire with cape, banderillas, and muleta quite
large enough to justify his equable conceit. He received his alternativa in 1944 at La Coruña, and had it confirmed in Madrid
the following summer. His immediate junior, who would enter on
the extreme right, was José María Martorell, a full matador since
1949: long-nosed, broad-shouldered, and generally accepted as the
most competent torero to have come out of Córdoba since
Manolete. I had seen Dominguín and Martorell before: between
them in the paseo would be two faces new to me. One was Isidro
Marín, a local hero from Tudela, who had taken the alternativa
in 1951 but had not yet fought as a matador in Madrid. The other
was the third son of the ex-matador Niño de la Palma: the official
protégé of Luis Miguel and the unofficial candidate for the highest
honors of the 1952 season, his first as a full doctor of tauromachy.
He was one of the sights I came to Spain to see: the suave young
star of Ronda, Antonio Ordóñez.

At this point my diary takes over the narrative:

"My first glimpse of Ordóñez as the bugle bleats and the four matadors start that firm, swinging walk across the sand, each with his cuadrilla in file behind him. Photographers fizzing and clicking away; banderilleros looking as glum as ever, picadors as surly. I see Ordóñez's face as the parade reaches the barrera beneath the president's box; he presses down his montera in the traditional way. It is a round unformed mug, which might belong to what the Americans call a 'drugstore cowboy.' He is nineteen years old, and wouldn't seem out of place drinking soda pop, pinching co-ed cheeks and piping, 'Drop dead!' As with many toreros, one can't imagine him the agent of adult emotion: how can this boy don nobility? Granted his courage, where will he find the control and intelligence to mold it into art? I am, as always when returning to the bulls after an absence, frankly incredulous. I survey the sheen of the percale and the glitter of the braiding, and feel another familiar sensation, this time of unreality. It seems fantastic that these men, a riot of ceremonial silks in pastel shades, should be party to a plan for meeting and killing a fighting bull. They belong in a different world, a circus world; you expect them to hold out hoops for a spry little dog in a ruff to jump through. Their ambience is one of festival gaiety, pantomime artifice; yet in it eight virgin bulls must be taught their place. The tempering of the bull's fury to the man's brisk skill, which is on the face of it impossible, makes up the wonder of the bullfight.

"My seat, a *barrera de sombra*, has cost me £3. It overlooks the *callejón*, the passageway between the audience and the red-painted wooden fence which separates the toreros, press, police, and bull-ring staff from the bull. Below me, the peons flare their capes, testing them. No need for water to damp and weight them against wind;

the air shakes with heat. 'Agua!' says Luis Miguel Dominguín to his
swordhandler, who gives him a drinking jug. He takes a mouthful,
rolls it round his mouth, and spits it out. Martorell sits brooding;
Marín brags to a friend in barreras. Ordóñez leans on the fence, his
soft mouth slightly open, looking vacant. Four amateur bands over
on the sunny side play like madmen, each trying to outblow the
others, but none drowning the noise of the crowd. The plaza is full
to the flag, and reeks of cheap scent and cheaper cigars. The smell
is the worst thing, sleazy and sinful. Then the bugle again; a momentary, universal pause in mid-breath; followed by a universal 'Ahhh!'
as the first bull trots into the sun.

"He quickly proves himself awkward and unmanageable, un-
responsive to any of Luis Miguel's ruses. No one is more expert than
Luis Miguel at the game of making a difficult bull look like a bad
bull, thereby deceiving the public; but not even his repertory can
cope with a bull which is both difficult and bad. And, anyway, he
looks listless. So far this season he has averaged three corridas a week,
which is too many, even for a maestro. On this occasion his picadors
save labor for him, on instructions, by destroying the bull before the
banderillas are placed. (I want to remind myself, in a spirit of sheer
nostalgia, of the rules of picking. First, the pick must not penetrate
beyond the circular disc four inches from the point; second, the
picador must await the bull's charge and not provoke it; third, he
must not twist the pick in the wound; fourth, he must not place it
in the same wound twice; fifth, he must not indulge in the maneuver
derisively called the carioca, whereby the picador keeps pivoting to
the right, preventing the bull from leaving the horse and forcing it to
go on taking punishment. I have rarely seen more than two of these
rules observed in any one bullfight; themselves cynics, the picadors
create cynicism around them. One school of thought would like to

see them banished altogether, and some other means introduced of testing the bull's caste and weakening its tossing muscle. I can't go as far as that. A pick correctly placed, with the man leaning over and the bull straining upward at the horse, makes one of the most stirring groups in the whole fight. The bull who insists under the prick looks as noble as Atlas. Later, he comes to resemble Mars. Unless, that is, his bravery is sapped, when he looks like Saturn, the symbol of leaden things.)

"Luis Miguel, having watched his bull bled by his myrmidons, declines to put in the banderillas himself; the crowd grumbles. He goes out, smiling loftily, tilting his boyish head back, with the sword and cloth. A trifle abstractedly, he tries some of the facile, perfect passes which his artistry permits of him. But there is no tension, no enmity in what he does. Watching him closely, I decide that, given such sensitive reflexes and such an uncanny ability to run backward without forfeiting grace, it is unthinkable that a horn should ever catch him.* Too much skill militates against the drama of the bullfight. Even when Luis Miguel really exposes himself—and I have seen him do so with immense bravery and style—it is hard to believe that he is not merely demonstrating another trick of trompe-l'oeil; like the fake medium in Gian-Carlo Menotti's opera, who finds when she materializes something real and frightening that it is indistinguishable to the world from her previous deceptions. At what point, I wonder, does the art that conceals art become the art that reveals art? At the point when pride supersedes integrity.

"The maestro shakes the cloth and takes the bull through a few of his slow, long left-hand naturals, bending well over the horns as they pass. Noticing that this is a chopping creature, which halts in mid-charge, he abandons that gambit. He becomes mildly testy, and

---

* It did, though, the following winter at Caracas in Venezuela. Luis Miguel announced his retirement shortly afterward.

shows his annoyance in the only way he knows, by patronizing the
bull. He grins, slaps its flanks as it passes, strokes it; and even, when
it bluntly won't charge, kicks its muzzle with the toe of a slippered
foot. This kind of horseplay, applied to bulls, is Dominguín's worst
vice, and I rejoice when, seeing that even vulgarity won't work, he
goes to the kill, after a faena lasting only six minutes. And how
atrociously he kills! He has the technique for a perfect volapié, but
rarely uses it, and this time it takes him five pinchazos and a media-
estocada to drop the bull. After which a *puntillero*, or daggerman,
has to finish the slumped animal off with a jab at the base of the
skull. Luis Miguel can do infinitely better than this, but he can also
do worse. I recall tales of a fight in Málaga, where the bull was so
heavily picked that when he placed the first pair of banderillas, one
of them slid into an open wound far enough to cut the aorta and
kill on the spot.

"It's worth dwelling on this first bull, if only to emphasize the
fact that the corrida bars none of the emotions. It differs from every
other minor art because of this emotional variety: the pendulum can
swing, in an instant, from extremes of shame and disgust to extremes
of exhilaration. If the fight is bad, you feel personally involved in a
stupid and slovenly fraud; if it is good, you feel cleansed and
ennobled—moved, even, to emulation. I doubt, in passing, whether
the local or the Madrid press will echo my opinion of Luis Miguel in
this first bull: the critics are predominantly his partisans, a clan
known as *Dominguistas*.

"Now follows a brief and bloody interlude with the Cordoban
Martorell, who cannot compete with the professor, Luis Miguel.
He is sincere, unspectactular and not without grace, but he lacks
one of the three classic qualities of the matador. He can stand his
ground (*parar*) and time his passes rhythmically (*templar*); but he

cannot *mandar*, which is to dominate and establish supremacy. Similarly, you might say of an actor that he had relaxation and good timing, but lacked authority. Martorell is graver than Luis Miguel, but his imagination rarely leads him out of safety. The great matador, like the great actor, must seem an unconstitutional, and therefore vulnerable, despot. Martorell's faena, with a bull which hooks and twists like a marlin, is safe and quickly over. The enemy—in Spanish journalism the bull is often *el enemigo*—won't follow him into the maze of intricate toil that makes a good fight, and he kills lamely and perfunctorily.

"Furore of expectation now for Ordóñez: it's his first fight in Pamplona and, as always, it may be his last. With every bull the good matador rehearses his last steps on earth, sketches the ceremony with which he will meet the last adversary. Most fighters escape the bulls unmaimed, and the statistics show that only one torero in twenty-five dies from their attentions; but the sentiment of peril is so overpowering that in every bullfight, no matter how bad, there is a quality of swan song. As Annabella says in John Ford's play:

> This banquet is an harbinger of death
> To you and me; resolve yourself it is,
> And be prepared to welcome it.

"But Ordóñez leaves us esurient. To begin with, his bull has one horn splintered at the tip, possibly the result of the practice of nocturnal horn-shaving which is the most glaring corruption of modern bullfighting. Next, it lollops like a great dog, whereas good bulls trot. Ordóñez pouts, shrugging with his lips, and, after a few idle passes with the cape, hands the unwieldy brute over to the picadors, who pick it to a comatose, blundering mess. With the muleta he is casual, but there are glimpses of real virtue in his work, reminding me of early pictures of Nicanor Villalta, the great bald Aragonese killer of the twenties, who would spin, tiptoe, with the bull as it passed, and whose knees, preposterously knocked, suggest a parody of Ordóñez's. Two or three right-hand naturals, gloriously protracted, show me that Ordóñez has mastered the art of 'running the hand'—i.e., following through, using the full length of your arm to elongate the pass until the bull's tail is almost passing your stomach. Only five minutes of faena, and a quick, cowardly kill, running in a wide arc around the horns: the crowd buzzing, meanwhile, with protest. An inauspicious debut.

"The fourth bull belongs to Isidro Marín, whose friends from Tudela are here in force, cheering him as soon as Ordóñez has retired into the callejón, and brandishing a banner which reads: 'Salutations and amity to Isidro Marín, the courageous matador of our township.' Certainly he looks brave, in a stocky way, and the deep scar on his left cheek did not come from shaving. At twenty-four, he is older than Ordóñez and Martorell, but I do not think he will ever rival them. Today he is trying hard because of local attachments, and in his first bull proves himself pugnacious, persistent, rock-steady—possessed, in fact, of the best qualities of industry without imagination. In the morning's *apartado*, at which the bulls are paired off and their numbers written on scraps of paper to be picked from a hat by the matador's representative, he drew the best couple. With his first he deals honorably, and is clearly willing to try anything anyone else has ever tried in a bullring, though not quite so effectively. Style is a stranger within his gates. In bull-fighting as in other arts, style can easily degenerate into prettiness, just as charm in a writer can putresce into ingratiation; but it must be there before we can salute a great torero.

"The bull, a very big one, is picked supremely well, high up but not too punishingly, by a battered old picador who must be over fifty. Now Marín embarks on an ambitious faena. He begins, as he should, with a statuary pass: feet together, the bull six yards from his left shoulder, both hands extended in front of him, presenting the sword and cloth as one instrument. A brusque shake of the muleta, and the bull charges, passing beneath it like an express train beneath one of the gauges used by the railways to limit the height of truckloads. He repeats this neatly several times, advances to left-hand naturals, and then surprises me with a resoundingly final chest pass. Well performed, it is one of the loveliest things in the repertoire, releasing the bull for a moment's respite like the uncoiling of a spring; or, to take a simile more precise, like the return to the tonic at the end of a cadenza. The bull is on the man's left, the muleta is in his left hand. He cites, and swings the cloth and the charge up past his chest, looking, as the horns push out from under the muleta, like a Herculean hunter with a monster on leash. Together with the natural, the chest pass is the touchstone of work with the muleta. Marín shines at it, as much as brass can ever shine, and then kills efficiently, but with no more emotion than a man who says: 'That's that.' However, the locals are enchanted, white handkerchiefs are waved in petition for a trophy, and the president awards Isidro two ears, which are cut off the bull by a peon, and handed to an *alguacil*, one of the two officials in black seventeenth-century garb whose job it is to see that the orders of the presidency are carried out. The alguacil gives Isidro his hairy prizes, with which he makes a tour of the ring. My own applause is tepid: one ear would have been ample reward.

"Luis Miguel's second bull is the vicious soloist of the morning's encierro, half a ton of defensive sulks. The maestro smiles loftily at

the animal, as one imagines Flaubert might have smiled if asked to
write a children's fairy tale, the smile of a stylist faced with a task
beneath him. Some wide, safe verónicas with the cape are followed
by a refusal on Luis Miguel's part to put the banderillas in himself;
this is a characteristic gesture of pettishness toward the crowd, whose
reaction to his first faena had been what the Spanish press calls
'division of opinion'—i.e. whistles drowning the applause. But with
the muleta he begins to teach the bull, intimately and with devotion, gently persuades a difficult, wide-horned creature to follow the
cloth, to regulate its speed of charge to his own speed of wrist and
reflexes. A fine, patient exhibition of his facile, rehearsed-looking
method, and an exemplary faena of the second rank; second, because the muleta never leaves Luis Miguel's right hand. Sixteen
close, steady right-hand naturals, not giving an inch to the bull,
followed by three lithe essays in the molinete, a right-handed pass
in which the torero spins on his heels against the bull's line of
approach, wrapping the cloth around his waist as he turns. The
crowd chimes in with 'o-o-olé!,' as we are treated to statuary passes,
high right-handed passes, and more molinetes. The kill is bungled, a
good half estocada needing three attempts to descabello before it is
completed.

"Let's forget Martorell's second bull, the sixth of the afternoon:
I whiled away the butchery by accepting too many glasses of sherry
from my neighbor, and eating greasy hunks of red Pamplona sau-
sage. The picking was atrociously inept, and so violent that only
one of three pairs of banderillas found anchor in the animal's hacked
withers. Martorell disgraced himself and dishonored his bull, and
all quite wittingly, as if neither we nor his adversary were worth his
trouble. This kind of proud obtuseness assails more matadors than it
should. He took the cloth, and, after feeling his way with some

tentative double-and-chop passes, down on one knee, he gave up and sighted along the sword for the kill.

"The crowd is by now an aviary of whistles—I wonder, by the way, how much misunderstanding of the bullfight is due to a failure to realize that in Spain a whistle is a mark of extreme disapproval, not of appreciation. How often I've heard this: 'The little dago couldn't kill the wretched creature, he just went on stabbing away, and the mob were going mad with blood lust, whistling and cheering. I said to Mary, I said . . .' The whistles for Martorell expressed the Spaniard's rooted contempt for a death which is neither clean nor quick. Clumsily, with growing inaccuracy, Martorell took sword after sword; I counted ten attempts to kill, between each of which there was the same ugly pause as the bull was lined up again in the correct attitude, hindlegs slightly apart, forelegs together. So protracted was the business that the president signaled with his handkerchief, and a trumpet blast was blown: Martorell had suffered the indignity of hearing an *aviso*, a warning that his faena had passed the prescribed limit of ten minutes. After thirteen minutes, there would have been a second blast, and after fifteen a third; the bull would then have been escorted by steers from the ring and dispatched outside. Martorell managed to finish the job before the second blew, but he was weeping as he re-entered the callejón.* Avisos are invariably reported in the press, and too many of them can ruin a bullfighter's career. They are badges of failure; because they mean that the man, like a pupil at an examination, has failed to solve the set problem in the required time.

"Ordóñez came out for the seventh bull with his lips tightened, feigning indifference to the outcome but squinting hard as the peons ran the animal for him. Luis Miguel tapped his shoulder and

* See Plate 53.

whispered grave advice in his ear, gesturing with his right hand like
a sculptor, whereupon Ordóñez ran steadily out and made the bull
a present of three low, late, leisurely verónicas, standing with his legs
apart, stiff at the knees, in the manner which belongs to Ronda and
is more commanding, though less slick, than the feet-together style
which one associates with Seville. After two light picks and one
pair of banderillas, he changed the acts, and cantered out into the
middle of the ring, confidently, to dedicate the bull to us all, an ever-
popular gesture made by removing the montera, swinging it at
arm's length through a slow wide arc, and then dropping it onto
the sand. Warily hitching his trousers up, he shook the muleta, took
a grip on the sword, and cat-footedly lined the bull up for a breathless series of linked passes, first with the right hand, then with the
left—about thirty in all, textbook tauromachy, simple and brave.
He greeted the olés with a slack little smile, and killed ignobly, two
swords hitting bone before the third entered the lung. He was
granted an ear, and with it toured the ring in a shower of hats, coats,
wineskins, cigars, handbags and binoculars. When he returned to
the callejón Luis Miguel patted him on the back, but I was glad to
see that he only winced, frowned, and shook his head.

"Isidro Marín in the last bull did all he could within his intel-
lectual and physical limitations, which are considerable. Slowly,
piling pass on pass, he accumulated (it is the only word) a faena of
fantastic elaboration and little shape. To see Marín performing
such delicacies as the kneeling molinete, the manoletina, or the
dosantina (a sort of Alfred Lunt pass, in which the torero cites the
bull with his back) is something like hearing one's favorite bits of
Pope on the lips of a traffic policeman. Even so, it was a rigorous
exercise for him, and all the more daring because, technically, he
was not really up to it. Two ears were a fair tribute: all the same,

I would rather see Ordóñez cut one. Ordóñez, even at half pressure, makes a knightly narrative, a medieval *roman* of chivalry, out of the corrida; Marín is the prose translation, for use in schools. He is a splendid crib: no more. Until, that is, he goes in to kill: here he beats Ordóñez hollow. Ordóñez could not have rivaled the mighty, arrogant estocada with which Marín disposed of his second bull: it flashed in the air, and vanished up to the hilt, with real peril and majesty in it, the left hand steering the horns away from the body to the right, and the right hand crossing over and downward with the steel. I thought of Beddoes: 'Let heaven unscabbard each star-hilted lightning.' I have seen few kills more staunchly lethal, save in old pictures of Luis Freg. Marín was set on by a mob of boys, carried shoulder high in a delirium of glee around the ring and out into the shaded streets, with someone's umbrella brandished ludicrously over his head.*

"In the press on the way out of the ring, I found myself alongside Mme. Cartier-Bresson, the wife of the photographer, and asked her how she had enjoyed the fight. I could have bitten my tongue immediately afterward; I had forgotten that she is a Hindu, for whom the bull is the object of ultimate reverence. She looked at me impassively, pursing her lips. At length, quite lightly, she said: 'I think I understand. This is your revenge. Western Europe revenging itself on the East. Very well. Man kills bull—so Shiva creates the atom bomb.' She was not angry: it was merely that her profoundest suspicions about the Occident had been confirmed. She added that, of course, she would never again enter a bullring, and that she proposed to light a candle every afternoon in the cathedral for each bull that was marked down for slaughter. I believe she will, too. It had not been a good corrida: just as there is nothing more

* See Plate 54.

vulgar than a coarse religious painting, so there is nothing more awful than a bad bullfight. But there was no point in explaining."

The afición in Pamplona were not particularly downcast. The talk at the Café Chóko was loud in praise of Marín's second estocada, and the courage with which he took a bump with the flat of the horn as he delivered it.* He had been thrown to the ground, and the bull turned and trampled him, so that the danger was real and close for a moment, until capes were flashed under the muzzle: whereupon, satisfactorily, the bull crumpled and died. I found myself pondering with more and more pleasure the glimpses I had seen of Ordóñez's quality. Already I saw in him the laziness of the true perfectionist. He is not the kind of artist from whom emotion pours, rough and jagged and unsightly, this way, that way, in a hot cascade. He is clearly a victim of moods; a good one swept over him briefly during the second bull, and one could almost sense him thinking: "How if I polish this pass, soften its crudeness, lengthen its rhythm, bring up its high lights, make it a complete experience?" Before your eyes Ordóñez purifies his craft, taking all the pains of a master jeweler at work on a precious stone. There are bullfighters who are at their best when improvising, but Ordóñez is not one of them. He is an interior vision of an ideal faena, and each of his faenas brings him nearer to realizing it. With the bull who is intractable, who will not conform to the ideal, Ordóñez has no patience at all. He relapses into the apathy of a first-rate artist tackling a job which he knows cannot possibly produce better than second-rate results.

The second corrida, with light Sancho Fabres bulls, was a fascinating calamity, a gray afternoon of squalor and incompetence,

* This estocada and what followed it are illustrated in Plates 48 and 49.

relieved in the last ten minutes by a blaze of achievement. What is the right word when shame and depression fuse into a new and indivisible emotion? The first five fights that afternoon provoked it, whatever it is, leaving me with the sensation of having sought sin and not enjoyed it. The sin, perhaps, is accidie, sloth and disgust and black fingernails whirlpooled together. When a bullfight, with everything conspiring to make it memorable, decides to fail, then for hours afterward one slackens, gives up, concludes that nothing can ever succeed. After five bulls had been killed without honor, I ceased even to feel the lift of expectation as the new bull entered and made its first, fast, waddling thrusts at the cape. The matadors were Manolo González, the twenty-two-year-old Sevillian who in 1951 took part in more corridas than anyone except Luis Miguel himself; Martorell; and Manolo Vázquez, younger brother of the capricious, adulated, semi-retired Pepe Luis Vázquez, who nowadays seems to have lost interest in the profession which, according to all reports, he could easily have dominated. Manolo Vázquez, in his first season as full matador, is a depraved-looking, ugly, slit-eyed little man, who fights with true Sevillian panache and is managed by Marcial Lalanda, the finest journeyman torero of the thirties. González has a simple style, almost smug in its purity, but he lacks ambition. He took his doctorate at Seville in the spring of 1948, after a riotously successful career as novillero. Since then his decline has been steady, almost deliberate; his modest pug face seldom lights up with anything more potent than the simple wish to be in good health for his next airplane trip to Mexico. In the *dégringolade* of most good matadors, such as the gypsies El Gallo and Cagancho, there is a weird, tessellated charm; they are metamorphosed from sonneteers into wits, and even in their torpor and cynicism flashes of the lyric inventiveness of their best days remain. González has declined ungracefully into numbness; a less prepossessing advertisement for the Sevillian style could scarcely be imagined.

Unluckily, he drew the two heaviest bulls; more unluckily still, a high wind was blowing. With his first he made a token effort at cape-work; the passes had a fine sweep and amplitude, and Manolo flashed the cape, as always, like a carpet shaken to release dust. But he shunned proximity to the bull, intimidated by its size, and the picadors punished it severely; it came plodding to the kill, and the whole fight was over, picks, sticks, and sword, in ten minutes. The second took eleven minutes, and in both faenas he restricted himself to a few double-and-chop passes and a safe, unpretty kill.

Martorell, who took the second and fifth bulls, was dull and empty of ideas, doing nothing to rebuild yesterday's ruins. Both his bulls were comically eccentric: the crowd laughed at them. The first was a wayward lightweight, with a marked penchant for sitting down, like a Disney fiction, and sniffing the tobacco-scented air. The second was the most awkward of all combatants, the almost-human bull, with intolerably keen eyesight and a retentive memory, black as sin and wicked in its hooking, always following the man, not the cape, and refusing to charge until the man was practically between the horns. The bullfight, which is designed to exploit the courage of the brute, disintegrates if the brute acquires any human qualities—cunning, guile, or the rudiments of imagination; when this happens, the antithesis of the spectacle is destroyed. Martorell's second bull outwitted him all the way, and it was absurd to see the creature stalking huffily away from the matador, who trotted after it in rising spleen twice round the ring. The picadors plunged in, and one of them was fined 250 pesetas for overenthusiasm; the president called for the arrow-tipped black banderillas, but even they could not stir this overfed coward. The faena was ludicrously botched: Martorell dangled the muleta like a man tempting a donkey with a carrot, holding it so far away from his body that twice he almost overbalanced. The kill was abominable; I could swear he did it with his eyes shut; and both bull and matador, whistled to the echo, were accused of bastardy, drug taking, and perversions of every kind.

Then what is it about bullfighting, after all? Where is the delight? Isn't it an expense of spirit in a waste of shame to write about it? After Martorell's second bull I almost gave up. Even Vázquez, in his first, had been wretched; the little man did nothing with the cape, and made a clumsy faena worse by losing one of his slippers in the course of it; this had looked to be the best bull of the day, and as it sank to the sand after a cheap, slantwise estocada, wearing the banderillas like a festive shawl, I was on the verge of bequeathing my tickets for the rest of the feria to the hotel barman. But in his second, the last of the corrida, he brought me to my feet in an effort to catch my heart before it flew out of my mouth. It was a little bull, weighing only 565 pounds, but it was the right size for Vázquez and for the glory of bullfighting.

The crowd was unsettled throughout the first two acts of the fight. The gaitas played while the banderillas were going in, their tune being described by an Englishman behind me as "an old Navarrese lament"; it was actually "Mademoiselle de Paris." By the time Vázquez walked out into the wind and dedicated to us, the arena was emptying fast. He began modishly, citing from about ten yards and presenting both shoulders to the bull, not simply his profile. A man in profile can bend at the hips if the horns come too close; the man standing square on has less chance of cheating. The battle between the two schools is still unresolved, though nobody denies that the two-eyed stance is more ancient, and permits the torero to provoke the charge with his body and then use the muleta to take the bull off its course (cargar la suerte), thereby demonstrating his mastery more completely than the profiling method allows. Claude Popelin says of the profiler in his excellent book of theory, Le Taureau et son Combat, that "il a supprimé l'oblique, le cargar la suerte, le détour imposé en plein charge de la bête. Il ne la fait plus passer, il la laisse défiler. . . . En deux mots, on joue plus, on se bat moins."

The history of profiling is accurately summed up in a few pages later: "Les matadors ont torée de face jusqu'à Belmonte (1914), de trois quarts jusqu'à Manolete (1939), et, ensuite, de profil. Un tel abus de la position de profil a suivi l'exemple de Manolete qu'-aujourd'hui les jeunes toreros en vedette (Antonio Ordóñez, Manolo Vázquez, par exemple) reviennent tous plus ou moins au toreo de trois quarts, comme à une nouveauté."

Vázquez's first group of six left-hand naturals would have delighted M. Popelin: authoritative, changing the route, and beautifully followed through. Economical, too; in bullfighting economy of movement is a part of aesthetics, and Vázquez, having chosen his ground, held it and did not skip, shuffle, or step back between passes, as less scientific bullfighters will. The chest pass at the end of his series was a flaw, a vulgarity at the end of an epigram, for the bull jogged him and he almost stumbled; so, with enormous aplomb, the entire sequence must be repeated for us, six more left-handed sweeps with the body turning slowly on its axis like a statue in a modern museum. The crowd, forced by now into self-forgetfulness, was one voice rapt in the rhythm of the olés. Next, four mano-letinas, during the last of which the perilous thing happened: the bull halted halfway through the pass with its right horn an inch from Vázquez's armpit. He moved not at all, and there were five seconds of desperation to elapse before he gently shook the cloth;

the cameras, as it were, turned again, and the pass was accomplished.

A repertory of molinetes and kikirikis followed, and a final, imperious chest pass, after which Vázquez turned to kill, and turned much too soon; for the bull turned with him, like a dog after its master, and caught him a great stab in the thigh. Down he went, somersaulting, the bull on top of him in a flash, rolling him in the sand and punting him with the horn feet into the air. The peons were in with their capes as he leaped up, sore and stricken with anger, and ordered them from the ring. Rabidly he profiled and went straight in to kill, his braid all torn and dangling; and there was no need for the attendant's dagger to finish off the job. Vázquez and his bull had grown together in dignity as the fight progressed, and he killed at their joint peak, quite perfectly. The award of both ears was automatic.

Fifty years ago bulls used to be matched in Spanish rings with imported lions and tigers (which they always defeated), just as nowadays heavyweight boxers fight other heavyweight boxers. As Vázquez stood with hand upraised over what he had killed, he might have been a symbol of the majesty of unequal combat, where the end is fixed and only the path to it unknown, and where, in consequence, art is within the frontiers of possibility.

One of the bullfight's greatest enemies is the intense romantic. It is in many ways a pity that most of the books which have brought bullfighting to the English language (I except Hemingway's, still the soundest and best) have been written in a state of literary *kif*. This kind of thing: "A dark, swelling knot tightened within José's gut. This was it, then, this was what men called fear and looked away. Mother of God, he needed another *anís*, how bad he needed it. His gut was a flapping, empty wineskin, like a man should not have if he

is killing bulls. And he was out there alone with it, alone with the
horned fury. Little Saint Penelope of the lollipops, but that Number 28 was an *ayuntamiento* with sabres, a bitch of a bull. I got to
tie the bastard down, crooned José within himself, I got to make
beauty of the bastard. He went toward the horns, walking on fire
and sick to his stomach. 'Thou art my toro, thou son of a tart,' he
whispered in Spanish. 'This is my afternoon and thou art my art. O
thou noble bull of Andalucía, be good to me and be not a pigeon
dropping.' After his first series of seventy-eight linked naturals with
the left, the true and honest hand, he felt better. The dark knot was
cut, a great passion came in upon him, and his blood flowed in mys-
tic surges. The hilt was burning him, the hilt of the sacrificial spear.
'Kill now,' said the soul of José el Rubio, 'kill now, and let it be
beautiful, that the old men may talk about it over their manzanillas
in time to come.' Uhh-hah, Señor Toro, I am ready for you, you
chicken pellet, said José el Rubio, and he straightened his old man's
shoulders and he took the black bulk of the most noble bull of all
the Conde's pastures full on the point of his singing sword. 'Was it
well done?' he shouted to his peasant of confidence. 'Was it well
done, Pepe?' And Pepe showed him his young man's thumb and
said that yes, it was well done, it was well done indeed. . . ."

This kind of thing deforms the bullfight, presenting it as the
dream of a neurotic solipsist, substituting a phony ecstasy for the
stronger, sterner excitement of the reality. It makes the aesthetic
error of identifying the torero with his job, just as bad dramatic
critics will identify an actress with her parts: "And then, her wits
awry with sorrow at the death of her father, Miss Bartlett appeared
decked in flowers, poor woodland tokens of homage, and sang the
sad, ribald, remembered songs of her infancy. . . ." To sentimenta-
lize the bullfight is to commit a crime against it. For its finest

moments bullfighting depends on restraint and Olympian detachment, never on what Landor called "the hot, uncontrollable harlotry
of a flaunting dishevelled invention." When the fighter is at his
coolest, the emotion is often at its height. The fight is a romantic
spectacle, but its practice is a science. I am pretty sure there were no
supernatural communings going on within Vázquez as he killed his
bull. Rather the contrary: the dapper coldness, the hair's-breadth
certainty of what he did gave it the quality of heroism which made
it memorable. You do not climb Everest singing hymns.

3

Litri

THE most discussed matador on the peninsula arrived at my hotel that night: Miguel Báez "Litri," who deserves grateful introduction, because it is to him and the strange starveling power he displayed in the summer of 1950 that I owe the inception of my interest in bullfighting. He lives in Huelva, a small mining port seventy miles from Seville, set about with ranches whose bulls may be glimpsed from the road, grazing in ponderous silhouette. The journey there springs for a few yards into fantasy, at the crossing of the Rio Tinto, which runs crimson and gold over rich surface deposits of copper. Huelva is fetid and tourist-scorned, though transient sailors prize it for its tidy red-light district, where there is a bar whose proprietor, a defaulting poet, knows most of Ben Jonson by heart.

The town has four heroes, three of them dead. One is the nameless corpse, celebrated in Duff Cooper's *Operation Heartbreak*, which floated ashore at Huelva bearing forged information which embarrassingly misled the Germans about the Allied plans for invading southern Europe. Another is Columbus, who sailed westward from the estuary of the red river where his statue towers, staring quizzically at the sea. The third idol, a lean torero christened Manuel Báez and professionally nicknamed "Litri," was killed in

1926; and the fourth is my Litri, Manuel's half brother, who out-weighs, in local and national esteem, all the other attributes of Huelva put together. I have no doubt that when Columbus crum-bles, the street boys will still be chalking "VIVA EL LITRI" on the walls of the town hall, and others after them will be adorning the inscription with forests of what the Spanish call admiration marks; for Litri is the marvelous boy who decided in 1952, the season of which I am writing, against perishing in his prime, and accordingly gave up fighting bulls. He announced his impending retirement two months after the Pamplona feria; he was then twenty-one and had put together in four sudorific years a fortune of twenty-five million pesetas, which is about $700,000. In Spain, where the return on capital is exceptionally high, that is very rich indeed. Week in, week out, few people on earth earn more than a popular matador; he can command up to $7,500 for an afternoon's work; but Litri alone among the millionaire swordsmen can claim to have been a national hero at nineteen and a national enigma at twenty-two. When he retired, speculation about his future became something of a na-tional pastime; one recalls similar curiosity about Garbo when her name vanished from the marquees. The cafés of Andalusia echoed with argument, as loud voices insisted that he would and would not return to the ring, that he would surely marry an actress, that on the contrary he would become a monk. The rumors about him were and are luridly diverse, and the truth is strange enough.

I saw him first in 1950, and often in the two years that followed. He was without question a highly original performer, stormy and intense, though extremely limited in his repertoire: a true *torero corto*, or short bullfighter. With the cape he would be valiant one moment and grotesque the next; the excitement he communicated depended mostly on the muleta, and specifically on two peculiar passes. For one of them he would skip thirty yards away from the horns and take the charge from that ridiculous distance. Holding the muleta behind him with both hands, as if drying his legs after a shower, he would stand stock-still until the bull was almost upon him and moving fast, when he would deflect the horns with a leisurely flourish of the left hand. This always bound a spell, and was as often accused of showiness as his second trick, which was quite simply to ignore the bull as it passed by his body; to stare away —not at the crowd (Manolete had done that) but up at the sky, as if inviting a thunderbolt. Litri knew how to perform most of the basic passes with the muleta, but it was his twin innovations that sold the tickets.

His father, Miguel Báez, was a stout fighter of the old school who appeared in the inaugural bullfight at the Huelva Plaza de Toros in 1902. Deficient in finesse, often and savagely punished by the bulls, he is remembered chiefly as a strong, clean killer. His first son Manuel followed him into the ring in 1923. This was the "brown-faced, bow-legged little boy with black hair" whom Hemingway describes in *Death in the Afternoon*: "A prodigy of valor and wonderful reflexes, but insensate in his bravery and very ignorant in his fighting." I never saw Manuel, but this is Miguel to the life; the old man somehow transmitted a crazy frailty to both his sons. In 1925 Manuel won the Golden Ear trophy at Madrid against stiff competition, and met a girl in Valencia whom he determined to marry. Publicly and privately he seemed to be thriving, when a galling complication intervened. He brought his sweetheart to Huelva, and his father, a recent widower, fell in love with her— immediately, violently and inconsolably. A bizarre triangle seemed imminent; but the solution arrived before the situation had time to develop. In February, 1926, a bull's horn found Manuel at Málaga and ripped through his right leg. The wound turned gangrenous as a result of faulty surgery, and amputation, the bullfighter's death knell, had to be performed. It was as much from professional despair as from injury that Manuel cried out and died.

After a decent period of mourning, the old man married his dead son's fiancée. Miguel, who was born in October, 1930, is the child of that haunted marriage and of his father's sixtieth year; fifteen months later his young mother was widowed. Shortly afterward she gave birth to a daughter, thereby providing for Miguel an upbringing which could scarcely fail to produce abnormal results—he lived among women, with a mother twice bereaved, in a poor home where he was the only breadwinner. The qualities of overmothered children, shyness, quick resentments, passionate cleanliness, guilt feelings, defiant independence, were early implanted in him; his childhood friends remember him as being always "absent" in his demeanor, moody and distrait. He left school at thirteen, disrelishing study, whereupon his mother began to indicate her hopes that he might, like her father, become a railway clerk; anything to preserve him from the bulls. He made no comment. When he was fifteen she was shocked to learn, from a friend who assumed she knew already, that Miguel was spending all his spare time practicing. What kind of practicing? With young cows, said the friend, on the ranches; practicing bullfighting. Before long he was intervening in capeas, village scrambles with yearling heifers, and in June, 1947, three months before his seventeenth birthday, he killed his first bull at a country fight near Huelva. His mother tried to numb the sore part of her memory, and in the five ensuing years she never once saw him fight, never dared even to listen to the radio commentaries. In 1948 he fought a dozen times, with moderate success, as an obscure novillero. It is a safe bet that no one who saw him guessed that within a year he would ride in triumph across Spain and make bullfighting history.

In the ten months from February to November, 1949, Litri broke a record which had lasted thirty years. In 1919 Belmonte took part in 109 fights; Litri's tally for the 1949 season was 115.* Fighting three or four times a week, crossing and recrossing the country in dusty and fatiguing overnight journeys, he had the most successful year in all the chronicles of the corrida; his trophies totaled 225 ears, 68 tails and 31 hoofs. Huelva was systematically deafened by his admirers, who called him El Atómico and boasted explosively by letting off a firecracker for every ear he cut. He was usually partnered by a young madrileño named Julio Aparicio, the perfect foil for him, a "long" bullfighter (torero largo) with a spectacular all-round canniness far beyond his years; Aparicio was to Litri what Lagartijo had been to Frascuelo and Joselito to Belmonte. Their campaign as novilleros continued in 1950, astutely managed by José Flores Camará, a specialist in "phenomenons" who had handled Manolete's affairs and whose trademark was a pair of dark glasses bequeathed to him by the great Cordoban. Controversy crackled around the two boys, and Camará assiduously encouraged it, knowing quite well the truth of Unamuno's remark that Spain is divided into two groups, Anti-Exers who believe in Z, and Anti-Zedders who believe in X. The negative precedes the positive in that land of extremists, where a man cheers only that which diametrically opposes something he detests. Aparicio was applauded for not being Litri, and vice versa; theirs was the familiar rivalry of the demonstrative extravert and the stony introvert. Already it was apparent that Litri was more of an enigma than most bullfighters. At nineteen he was

* In defense of Belmonte's prestige, it should be remembered that his fights were corridas, whereas Litri's were novilladas.

earning more than $20,000 a week, and it seemed to mean nothing
to him; between fights he brooded at home, unsmilingly playing
naïve card games with his friends or, clad in outsize gabardine suits,
staring with deep, accusing eyes at American comic books. Most
prosperous toreros either invade society or woo film stars, forms of
ostentation which Litri deplored. He was in the business of killing
bulls for reasons other than those of social or sexual conquest; private
reasons, at once incommunicable and immensely urgent.

He made his debut in the Las Ventas ring at Madrid on May
18, 1950. His first bull came out of the toril at 5:45 P.M.; at five
past six it was dead; but the intervening twenty minutes had passed
into legend. After his first series of left-hand naturals, the crowd of
23,000 was on its feet in uproar, throwing hats and flowers into the
arena in a display of enthusiasm unprecedented in the cathedral of
tauromachy, as unheard-of as applauding after the first movement of
a symphony. Litri did all the right, reputable things and all the
extravagantly wrong ones; "he seemed," noted one reporter, "to
be fighting in a hypnotic trance"; he brought off his two tricks to
perfection, delighted both the experts and the tourists by the speed
and valor of his kill, and was awarded both ears by unanimous
petition. Madrid thinks the tail a coarse and repellent trophy, and
hence never bestows it; but Litri's supporters in Huelva made up for
the omission by giving him a miniature tail of spun gold when he
returned home. At the end of the season he graduated to full
matador status, which meant that he would henceforth be matched
with the heavier four- and five-year-old animals. The critics shrugged
and began to sketch out obituaries for the young suicide.

In 1951, to their confusion, he was earning more than ever, just
as riskily, and was never dangerously gored. I saw him at the July
fair in Valencia with bulls of Carlos Nuñez, Antonio Urquijo, and

Juan Pedro Domecq, three strains he especially favors, since they have provided for him more straight-charging "bulls on wheels" than any other breeders. To many toreros the bull is an instrument to be played on, and it was Belmonte who said that bullfighting was an art for which the Stradivarius and the stock cadenza already existed; but to Litri the bull was always the enemy, something terrible and infinitely to be hated. He was never much afraid. "When I feel the horn going in," he told me in a rare burst of consecutive speech, "I just switch off, like an electric light."

That winter, preceded by a riotous and unfortunate blast of publicity, he made his first and last trip to Mexico. He was being paid more than Manolete; he must therefore be greater than Manolete—that, at any rate, was the assumption, and it angered the Mexican afición. Though he made a statement to the press denying that he was any kind of messiah, the damage had been done. Stung by what they took to be Spanish *amour-propre*, the crowd hooted him when he appeared in the capital, burned him in effigy and threw petrol-soaked cushions flaming into the ring. He canceled his remaining fights and returned shaken to Spain. A virus of insecurity seemed to have invaded his system, and the early part of the 1952 season was, for him, disquietingly erratic. Instability had crept into his style; his old aloofness seemed to have dwindled into absent-mindedness. Many good critics were saying openly that he was finished, and his performances at the two great bull fairs of July, Pamplona and Valencia, were obviously going to be crucial to his career. I went next day with fingers crossed.

He was on trial with Luis Miguel and Manolo Vázquez before six Domecq bulls, and, more dismally than I could have imagined, he failed. Of all the melee of emotions which a bullfight can evoke

—passion, fright, shame, and wonder among them—he was consistent only in shame. His picadors, acting under orders, were killing his bulls for him, turning the black muscles into velvet fountains, pumping crimson. He was outwardly unchanged. Litri has what Wilde saw in Max Beerbohm and called "the secret of perpetual old age"; he is gnomish, withdrawn and ancient, with an enormous nose and straw-thin calves. But last year's smoldering pride was somehow damped down. Why? The crowd made its opinion brutally clear: his wealth had made him lazy. "Go home, rich boy!" yelled my neighbor. "Try fighting Cadillacs!" Vázquez, his junior in the ring, showed him up badly, dominating without fear, ushering the bull past him as if through a revolving door. What made the debacle even worse was that Litri appeared almost unaware of it. He was found guilty as charged, and one would have sworn he had not heard the verdict.

The Domecq bulls were middle-sized, averaging 587 pounds en canal, not dangerously armed but slow and indirect in attack; the kind which charitable and corruptible Spanish critics describe as "disgracefully unsuited to the emotional style of the torero from Huelva." Luis Miguel, cool in the great heat, took the first bull out into *los medios*, the difficult and dramatic central part of the ring, which is farthest from help, and swung it through some fine verónicas. The first picador was badly tossed, falling under the horse and wrenching his knee, and there was a catching of breath until Vázquez came in with a superb quite. The faena was *echt* Luis Miguel, a steady, self-confident vindication of Blake's remark about mechanical excellence being the only vehicle of genius. He performed his kneeling molinetes and lazy desplantes like a conjuror explaining to an audience of children how the tricks are done, and killed casually with a half sword in the lung. Having, it seems, nothing more to learn, Luis Miguel can only teach, and the excitement to be derived from a lecture is necessarily limited. He cut an ear, and one applauded automatically but without burning the palms.

The picking of his second bull introduced that comparative rarity in modern bullfighting, competitive capework in quites; the three matadors taking turns to solve the same animal equation, and in so doing expressing their own personal equations. Luis Miguel's contribution was three kneeling *faroles*, blithe and flamboyant, with a fine flare of cape over his head. Then Litri, who was downright funny: he appears barely able to lift the cape these days, and his verónicas were as tentative as the attempts of a man to put a sack over the head of a berserk gorilla. Finally Vázquez, spinning like a top in four tight chicuelinas, welded bull, body, and cloth into the right density of composition. As a favor, Luis Miguel put the darts in himself, three lovely pairs. He first moistens his fingers in mid-ring, carelessly eying the bull, and then begins a long, loping, curving run, leading up to the still moment of incision before the horns, when the barbs drop in and the action is complete.

Luis Miguel does not go in for the gymnastics which Carlos Arruza favors with the sticks, the twisting figures-of-eight which change the bull's course twice or thrice, but he is athlete enough to encompass all the classic methods of insertion, including the tricky *de poder a poder*, in which the man uses the darts almost as a vaulting pole to carry him across the trajectory of the horns. His faena was *muy dominguista*, and reminded me of the cricketing expression about giving the ball plenty of air; Dominguín gives the muleta plenty of air, and holds the bull's muzzle to the cloth, drawing it forward at his will, as a slow bowler will lure a batsman out of his ground to the slaughter. The kill was indecent—four pinchazos and a crooked estocada—but the notices in the local papers conven-

Luis Vidal

18. Litri in trouble

19. A pick well placed by El Pimpi

Luis Vidal

Luis Vidal

20. A picador displaced: the matadors run in for the quite (left to right: Litri, González, Ordóñez)

Cartier-Bresson

21. Luis Miguel with banderillas: The preparation . . .

22. . . . . the action

Luis Vidal

23. Banderillas al quiebro by César Girón

Chapresto

24. Goring of a banderillero

Marin

25. Preliminary double-and-chop with the muleta (Ordóñez)

26. Chest-pass by Ordóñez

27. Carlos Arruza, against the barrera

VARIATIONS OF THE STATUARY PASS

28. Ordóñez, with his toes to his hat

29. The rigidity of Litri

**CONTRASTING NATURALS
AND A MOLINETE**

30. The suppleness of Ordóñez

31. Kneeling molinete by Carlos Arruza

32. High right-handed pass by Jesus Córdoba

33. A high, old-fashioned natural by Calerito

34. Dosantina by Chicuelo II

35. Manoletina by Julio Aparicio

GRACE-NOTES WITH THE MULETA

36. Afarolado by Jumillano

37. Arrucina by Pedrés

iently closed their eyes to it, and we were told, as always, that Luis Miguel gave "a veritable lesson in the art of tauromachy." Qui est le meilleur torero de l'époque? Luis Miguel, malheureusement.

Of Litri's work with his two bulls there is little to record. It was shocking: the vessel of his talent seemed to lie smashed at his feet, and when a bullfighter goes through a period of inner disintegration, it shows more painfully than in any other craft. The first bull, picked to ribbons, was incapacitated for the rest of the fight; and Litri dishonored it still more with the muleta. Or rather with four muletas, all of which were whisked out of his slack fingers on the horns as he tried his luck with right-hand naturals. Literally, as well as metaphorically, he had lost his grip.

Taking a fifth muleta, he ran to the sunny side, proposing to cite for his long-range pass. But this, like all the best tricks, exacts a ghastly penalty from the man who fails to bring it off: it makes him look stupid, not a failed hero but a fool. When the bull refused to charge, Litri was forced to trot back toward it in a derisive faint hail of catcalls, as if he had climbed to the top board, taken a bow, and then had to climb down for his bathing costume. Now at close quarters, he tries to persuade us that he is intent on giving us our money's worth. He stands with the muleta behind him, taunting the bull with barely perceptible thrusts of the hip, but behind each thrust is a pathetically obvious prayer that it will not charge at all, now or ever. So he exposes himself, stares balefully at the crowd, and exposes himself again; his whole technique rests on exposure, which is meaningless where there is no risk. It is as crude as insulting a waiter. At last he gave up, and one hoped this anatomy of inadequacy would end. Two indolent pinchazos prolonged it before, by sheer chance, he killed *a un tiempo*, which is the technical term used when the man and the bull charge each other, and the sword goes

home as they collide. It is not a bad way of killing, but any way is
bad that is accidental, and Litri has nothing like enough technique
to formulate and execute rare *suertes* like this one. Stoic in disaster
as in triumph, he walked back to the callejón and conversed with
Camará out of the corner of his mouth. He exerted himself even
less with his second bull, an extreme manso. With the muleta he
posed as before, with the same lack of effect, shrugging toward us,
like an actor who should explain, between the lines, that the script
is not really worthy of him. After a few minutes of this, guessing
rightly that we had had enough, he ran in a disgraceful quarter
circle and made a safe kill.

Vázquez could do nothing with his first, a hysteric of an animal
which showed its lack of caste by thrice leaping into the callejón
and scattering the police and press; the instinct to escape does not
exist in the toro bravo, because it is a sensible, human, and therefore unbullish quality. Double-and-chop with the muleta, and
Vázquez killed like lightning, washing his hands of the whole affair.
His second inspired Luis Miguel to a luminous *quite por gaoneras*,
and even brought Litri padding in with some idea of a verónica in
his head, but a burst of snake-pit hissing from the crowd abruptly
changed his mind. Vázquez's faena, politically aimed at the occu-
pants of the cheap seats, bore all those marks of care and concentration which distinguish him at anything like his best. Planted like
a tent peg, he extracted two series of wristy naturals from a bull
which was rapidly going onto the defensive; and when this happens,
you are watching conscientious bullfighting, blood being squeezed
from a stone, grace from leadenness. We heard real olés for the first
time in the afternoon, and when Vázquez rose from the kill, like a
glittering exclamation mark, the applause was a thanksgiving.
Because, nowadays, only long faenas reap two ears, Vázquez had to

be content with one. By contrast with Litri's showing, he deserved the whole carcass.

There is pathos in the spectacle of the child who has tried and failed to please; in that of the spoiled child who is careless whether he pleases or not there can be none. Litri's manner in the ring that day was that of the careless child. The eclipse of his valor was, even when you have made allowance for the intransigence of his bulls, dreadfully complete. Some etiolation of the spirit had depleted him; even the desire for applause had waned, as could be seen from the brusque, perfunctory nods of the head which were all his response to the few handclaps he earned. Whatever he had wanted to prove was proven; whatever mission had compelled him to the fantastic achievements of 1949 and 1950 was fulfilled; he was rich, he was whole, his debt to his mother was amply repaid. There was now about him a yearning for idleness and respite, a desire to evade the horns forever, to ride fast in expensive cars and breed the fighting cocks which, like so many toreros, he loves to watch. He, who had but one perfect faena and must always seek in patience the bull which would permit it, was learning the boredom of the actor who has played the same part for every night of a three-year run. The Pamplonicans were saying that he was afraid, but I do not believe that was true, except in the sense that all bullfighters are afraid. Time and triumphs had simply drained him of the need to fortify his insecurities with public approbation. I had recommended many of my friends to come to Pamplona to see Litri, and the experience must have taught them, as it forcibly taught me, that there is no consistency in bullfighting, and that all bullfighters more often disappoint than they delight. The torero is the only artist who works in public, improvising every time with bizarre and unfamiliar material, like the Saxon *scop*, whose job it was to reduce to the language of art the multiple clangor, the loose ends and incoherences of battle, and to do this extempore after supper in the chief's great hall. The torero's burden is greater, for if he fails we must blame him for the wasteful infliction of physical pain. That cloud was heavy over Litri after the events of the afternoon; and next day, I reflected sickly, a worse trial awaited him. He was to be matched, for the first time in Pamplona, with Antonio Ordóñez.

They had much to dispute, these two, the outgoing and incoming heroes of the season, and the fourth corrida had given rise to huge expectations. The bulls were of Atanasio Fernández, a breeder from Salamanca, where bulls are made to measure for individual toreros rather than for the fiesta as a whole, but I had seen them when they arrived three days before and came plunging out of their boxes into the corrals: handsome, heavy-headed and well equipped with horn. One especially impressed me, a solid gingerbread animal named Cigarreto which would have dressed out at something over 660 pounds. With these, surely, Ordóñez and Litri and even my *bête noire* González, the third on the cartel, could work a wonder or two.

There was no wind. A few spectator clouds hung unchivvied over the arena as we gathered for the fight. The only hint that the burning day might decline into disaster had come with the announcement, in an early edition of the evening paper, that foot-and-mouth disease had been confirmed among Don Atanasio's bulls, which had therefore been judged medically unfit for combat. So the Santa Casa de Misericordia, organizers of the fair, offered as replacements six bulls from the Sevillian ranch of the Marqués de Villamarta, whose green and gold ribbons can seldom have fluttered from creatures more comically inept. Sluggishly, pompously, they

followed each other into the ring, like prize bloodstock at an agricultural show. Two or three were jaunty, skipping away from the
capes and diving into the callejón like porpoises; and all were light-
weights. Litri and Ordóñez found themselves in the plight of
sculptors engaged to carve heroic groups out of slabs of blancmange,
while poor González could do nothing but abandon himself to
despair. He showed us the relics of a style once pure, but now
sweated away to a skeleton of itself. One of his banderilleros, a
short-winded bulldog of a man, received a wound in the thigh
while nailing a pair in the first bull, whereupon González decided,
if he had not done so already, to take a short cut to the kill: a
couple of derechazos, a quick chop or two, a wildly incompetent
estocada, and three attempts at the descabello. His second faena
was a blurred carbon copy of the first. So much, or so little, for
Manolo, stainer of *pundonor*.

The spectacle Litri presented was closer to tragedy in the pity
and terror it inspired in the more objective members of the audience. Here was a boy patently suffering from that terrible disease,
aesthetic amnesia; he had lost direction, forgotten his skills and the
reason for their existence, and the tools of his art no longer seemed
familiar and connected to him. The cape was an unmanageable
stranger, the muleta a foreign flag on a stick; it was like those dreams
in which one is forced to type an article on an octopus. The afición
excoriated him after the fight, explaining that his failure was due to
laziness, petulance, arrogance, personal loathing of Pamplona; even,
one undoubted slanderer hissed, to indulgence in drugs. Though I
felt as cheated as anybody, I could not withhold sympathy from
Litri; even saints must find life a treadmill when the power of
miracles is suddenly and capriciously withdrawn from them. There
was a nastiness in the ironic glee with which the crowd sang the

popular song *Olé Torero* in accompaniment to Litri's shocked, stumbling faenas, both of which contained moments of bravery insensate enough to make a man's reputation in any circus in Europe. But then that, I suppose, is one of the differences between the circus, where courage in the face of death is an end in itself, and the bullfight, where it is only a beginning.

At every step he took Litri was whistled, and sorrowfully many of them were away from the bull. His hands would not grip the cape, his feet twitched: it was his extremities which betrayed him, and he lacked the cunning to deceive the crowd, as Luis Miguel can, by timing his rearward steps so that nobody perceives them. His first *torito* behaved with all the fuss of a female impersonator. It tossed its head and shuffled away from trouble toward the spaces of sand unoccupied by its executioners. The picador had to give chase halfway round the ring before driving home, and then in a proscribed spot halfway down the spinal column. Attempting a chicuelina, Litri was prodded in the rump by the horn and sent flying. The faena might have been a good one if the bull had ever come within a yard of the matador's body. Once, during a chest pass, it did stagger within arm's length, and Litri shamefully shut his eyes tight, masking the danger. Four monumentally ill-judged manoletinas earned him a burst of sarcastic applause, which spurred him, shaking and sweating, to kill. The big, furious estocada which ended the fight passed unnoticed.

The last bull Litri fought at Pamplona was the fifth Villamarta, and a conclusive refutation of the Spanish saying that no fifth bull is bad. This one was bland, underweight, and a wanderer, as reluctant to accept a challenge as Litri was to offer one. The rage of the *sol* now touched the sombra. One gathered from the tumult that this had happened last year, too: Litri had come to the feria and departed in disgrace. The general rule that Andalusian bullfighters are never at their best north of Madrid was again being proved. "All we see of him that is good is in photographs!" screamed one man. "And I say they are all faked!" The bull veered away from the picks, lunged vaguely as the banderillas went in, and stood thereafter by the barrier, refusing to charge. At half-minute intervals Litri coaxed the dreaming, deadened animal into co-operating on a bad right-handed pass or two. In a stupor of desperation he even attempted his second trick, and gazed at the sky as the bull lumbered by, but the creature chanced to wag its head and knocked him ungracefully to the ground. Nobody felt compassion; each pass was greeted as a parody, with a roar of ferocious laughter. Cushions were plopping and thudding into the sand, in open defiance of the law, while some citizens cradled heavier missiles in their hands, perhaps recalling Belmonte's dictum that the decline of the corrida began when the ordinance was passed forbidding the throwing of bottles at bullfighters' heads.

Litri's face was gray, and trembling. His half brother, Manuel, had a nervous tic that killed him, for it affected his eyelids and made him blink in moments of danger. Miguel's tic drags down the corner of his mouth, so that he might be about to cry or to vomit. Thus he looked as he lined his timorous vagabond bull up for the sword, and it was terrible to watch. From my barrera seat, his estocada seemed a good one; and then the bull turned, and I saw why the boys on the sunny side were screaming obscenities. About four inches of sword-point shiningly protruded from the stomach wall. It took the maestro of Huelva three more attempts, in a crescendo of vituperation, to finish off the kill. He was hooted out of the arena, limping slightly, staring at his feet through half-shut eyes. The agony was over. We had seen what Herman Melville shuddered to describe: "the undraped spectacle of a valour-ruined man."

Ordóñez, whose first bull had lent itself to some gaudy capework but little else, now set about saving the afternoon. I doubt whether anyone alive could have done more, and if by the highest standards he failed, it was because five bad fights had left such a queasiness in our stomachs that we were no longer capable of digesting the soufflé. He met the last bull, named Baturro, with a *farol de rodillas* in the middle of the ring, and then, turning, repeated the gambit. We were off to a racing start, with all Ordóñez's lightness and felicity to give it impetus. Up on his feet, he administered six rounded verónicas as fine as any I have seen, low-swung and followed-through, and crowned these with a noble trio of gaoneras. This sequence of passes nailed down the coffin lid of Litri's reputation in the north; they exemplified all that he was not, stating unanswerably that buoyancy of spirit could dispel apathy in both bull and audience, and art vanquish ennui.

We all had the thrill of anticipation which rises when a matador scents a triumph; we shared his conviction that this was his bull, the gateway to his special apotheosis. Our impatience flowed through him, and after two picks he had the thirds changed, and again after one pair of banderillas. All thought of Litri was now banished. Taking the sword and muleta, Ordóñez made a popular dedication, sending his montera up to the box full of white-clad orphans from the Santa Casa de Misericordia: terrific applause. The sixth bull, like its predecessors, was a nomadic, unconcentrated animal, but by sheer diligence Ordóñez forced it into artistic focus: the mass was molded into shape, which is always a marvel, like watching mist clear over a crag, or a mystery become a fact.

Advancing all the time into the bull's terrain, he began with some smooth experimental derechazos, and then switched to the left hand, citing with his hip, stamping his foot, with his head thrown back

in hot-eyed derision. The bull, seeming slowly to realize its responsi-
bilities, followed the cloth eight times; and the music struck up as
Ordóñez finished the series with the splay-footed chest pass he loves,
and the impudent sword-swish across the bull's muzzle as he walks
away. We were hungry for more of this, but Ordóñez sensed that
the bull was tiring, and that the tension would shortly slacken.
Accordingly he went into a final spurt, a lightning selection of
decorative right-hand passes, fluently connected and crowded together like a fantasy of baroque. Four manoletinas of dazzling
rapidity; a desplante before the horns; and a flow of Ordóñez's
unique walking molinetes, for which he struts across the line of the
charge, spins between the horns, and emerges on the other side,
ready to repeat the maneuver. This part of the faena precisely simu-
lated the cock-and-hen dances of Spain, the two participants advancing formidably on each other, and passing without contact.
Before these lovely intersecting designs could pass from our minds,
he went in to kill; but the thrust went awry, and two more were
called for, two blots on the filigree pattern of his tracing, but not
enough to deprive him of an ear.

Whether Ordóñez is capable of the slow, sad fury of a perfect
bullfight I am not sure; his talent is wholly lyric, and though it can
turn out anything from occasional verse to sonnets it partakes not
all of the epic. His quality is *garbo*, defined to me in a letter by John
Marks, the doyen of English aficionados, as "animal grace sublimated
—the flaunting of an assured natural charm, poise infected by *joie
de vivre*, innate, high-spirited, controlled, the essentially female
attribute (even in bullfighters) yet far removed from sex appeal . . .
a zestful panache without vulgarity. Grace, a lithe grace, a lithe,
devil-may-care grace that hits the nail on the head, really and happily,
with no more than the precisely appropriate eye-filling flourish."

Ordóñez has it, he adds, and everything else but guts, for which the Spanish use an earthier expression; but it may be, as an influential Madrid weekly said recently, that there is too much emphasis on guts, melancholy and tragic dominion in modern bullfighting, and too little on the *garbo* of Ordóñez in his best days.

Escaping from the nervous debauch of the corridas, I visited a nearby *frontón*, or pelota court. This lethal game, a cracking, reverberating variant of squash played at ice-hockey speed with a ball solid enough to split a skull, has become so stratified that no amateur, however talented, could hope to defeat the least competent professional; it is the property and the prerogative of the great Basque athletes, who play it in family dynasties, sweeping all outside competition curtly from the courts. A frontón is normally a noisy place, filled with the uproar of frenetic betting, but this one was comparatively peaceful; a concourse of regional dances was being held. If I had hoped for respite, a moment's immunity, a surcease of reflection that mortality is a frail state, I should have known better. Glee in Spain does not ignore death; it invites death to the party. No sooner was I seated than four barefoot dancers marched in, bearing on their shoulders a coffin, on which in the attitude of a corpse there lay a small, bald man, clad in top-hat and tail-coat. The pall bearers, grinning broadly, halted in the center of the court, whereat the small man leaped to his feet and danced on the coffin lid.

It was a harum-scarum measure, all fits and starts and pretended slips, a miracle of balance on the abyss's edge, a shorthand telescoping of the farce of human life; yet it had a shape, and the dancer kept faith with its rhythm to the end. When it was done, he removed his topper, closed his eyes, and fell prostrate once more. So short, one tritely felt, is the zenith of bullfighters. Perhaps they are dead before they start; or, at least, some part of them is dead, the part which we call discretion and which impels us to pass our lives in avoidance of danger, fear, and the chance of disgrace. Thus musing, I returned to the hotel. There, sitting alone at the bar, calm and kempt in an outsize windbreaker, was Litri. He was staring at a glass of mineral water, and when I left, twenty minutes later, he had not moved a muscle.

Techniques are ductile things, and may change within a decade; but grand themes are immutable. The common denominator of all dramatic spectacles is a human being at the end of his tether; and this may well be the only absolute truth about drama, for it applies to all the kinds that the word covers. Lady Mulligan, in Tennessee Williams's play *Camino Real*, complains to Gutman, the proprietor of her hotel, that he has taken to sheltering some pretty undesirable guests; whereupon:

Gutman: They pay the price of admission the same as you.
Lady Mulligan: What price is that?
Gutman: Desperation!

It is the price of admission to all the inner sanctums of drama; the bruised individual soul must be driven, by logical and ineluctable process, to a state exactly definable only as one of desperation. This is the state reached by Oedipus, Lear, Hamlet, Othello, Solness, Hedda Gabler, Racine's Hermione, O'Casey's Juno, and all the other cornered giants of tragedy; it is reached, too, by the moribund gentry of Chekhov, as they retreat to their attics or huddle in their summer houses, while the storm gathers outside. *The Three Sisters* is a very epiphany of desperation. We may pride ourselves that we weep at the sight of desperate folk, but just as often we laugh at it. We laugh at Fancourt Babberley, forced to main-

tain his appalling imposture as Charley's Aunt; and the husband of
French farce, with a wife in one bedroom, a mistress in another,
and a mother-in-law halfway up the stairs—is he not, as he holds his
head in his hands and stares aghast at the heavens, a figure of fun?
Would *Love for Love* have quite the same comic impetus if the
hero, Valentine, were not so desperately, inextricably in debt?

At the heart of all fine plays, whether tragic or comic, a pool
whirls, sucking the characters down to confusion; and it is our
knowledge of this undercurrent which keeps us going to theaters.
The clown in the haunted house and the prince on the haunted
battlements are both desperate men, and as such equally eligible
for dramatic presentation. Anyone, in fact, who arrives at self-
knowledge through desperation is the raw material for a great play.
Its stature will depend on the honesty and art of the playwright,
but its cornerstone is already laid. And the rule holds good, though
we may not care to admit it, outside as well as inside the theater
or the film studio. The man in the dock at a murder trial exerts a
raw variant of the same steady, implacable charm as Oedipus; he
is called upon to answer the unanswerable, to breach the cul-de-sac;
he is facing what we could never face. And so, of course, is the bullfighter, the crystalline symbol of a classic plight, who must confront
and overcome the bearer of his own death. If he fails, as Litri
had failed, to measure up to the moment, he cannot console himself, as a man may who has been acquitted, with the thought that
the crisis has passed. Like a bad dream, the plight will recur, if not
the next day, then the day after.

Soon after dawn, with nobody to cheer or deride his departure,
Litri was driven off southward in a station wagon, accompanied by
his cuadrilla. I lost sight of him for two weeks thereafter, though

the reports of his performances which filtered through the national press were not encouraging. My next appointment with him was not until the fair of San Jaime at Valencia, when he and Ordóñez would meet to settle their account.

Meanwhile, with the four major fights over, Pamplona underwent a *relâche de détente*. The town spoke holiday, and the toreros joined in, wearing *traje campero*, tunics, tight pants, and Cordoban hats, for a benefit bullfight. Six novillos of Ignacio Sánchez y Sánchez were put to the sword quite lightheartedly; Luis Miguel and Ordóñez, his doting pupil, showed their skill in public relations by fighting in traditional Pamplonican costumes, Isidro Marín, the hero of the province, turned up with his elder brother Julián, and I got my first view of Calerito, the hawk-faced butcher from Cordoba who had just been admitted to the *grupo especial* of front-rank matadors. Bullfighters are annually graded, according to the salaries they command, by the national *Sindicato del Espectáculo*; in a normal year there are about twenty names in the special group, and thirty more divided among four inferior categories.

The charity fight was held in tree-whispering, lawn-mowing English summer weather, and one's impression was of a tipsy garden party. The bloodshed seemed properly incidental to the festivity. Everyone sang, the insomniac bands played, and all the fighters were automatically awarded ears; the president's box was occupied by five plump local beauties, and the *asesor*, whose job it is to advise the presidency what trophies it should concede, behaved with crazy generosity throughout the afternoon. The matadors responded to this genial treatment by attempting all the playful, ornamental passes at which the textbooks sneer. We saw, with the cape, such oddities as the *serpentina*, the *saltillera*, the kneeling verónica, and the *tapatía*; and with the muleta, the kikiriki and the arrucina—

all of them the sort of unproductive, exhibitionistic passes which
characterize country bullfights, where as a rule they are badly performed and result in gorings. To see these grace notes and curlicues
perfectly executed by virtuosi off duty was as instructive a delight
as watching literary lions playing parlor games or serious musicians
relaxing at a jam session.

Calerito alone approached his bull with a frown; he may have
been trying to live up to the dignity of his new status. Certainly he
cut an impressive figure, tall, bronzed, and weather-beaten, his
scowl and scars making him look older than his twenty-five years,
and one had to commiserate with him when the bull, a sloppy,
stumbling Salamancan black, refused to co-operate. The pastures
in that part of Spain seem to have an adverse effect on the animals'
forelegs, and this one, after submitting to a few right-hand passes,
firmly subsided to the sand, blew exhaustion through its nostrils,
and shook its head. Calerito cursed and gesticulated his contempt,
but to no purpose: the bull remained inert, like a great black
kitchen range on the verge of being dismantled. At length he
seized a horn and tugged it back to its feet. By a mighty effort of
will he guided it through a dozen simple passes, and then administered a bitter, fulminating *coup de grâce*.

He had displayed great willingness and considerable nobility;
yet in his nobility there had been something irrevocably clownish.
Calerito brings a whiff of the prizefight to the bullring. A bath-
robe, garishly initialed, would suit him better than the suit of
lights; he advances on the bull in the rolling gait of the cruiser-
weight contender marching into Madison Square Garden. One
feels, perhaps unfairly, that he relishes blood and buffeting, and
the feeling is reinforced by a trick of shaking hands with himself
at head height when he takes a bow.

This is not to deny his quality. The following day, in company with Isidro Marín and another second-class matador, Rafael Llorente, he revealed himself a torero of complete and undoubted accomplishment. Marín and Llorente fought bravely and killed well, but both were overshadowed by Calerito and his battered arrogance. His first Montalvo bull was a fine black-and-white flyer with plenty of weight, the day's champion by far. Its first action was to rip a peon's cape completely in two, which brought Calerito running out for a breathless bout of chicuelinas which beautifully modified the bull's impetus. These were the preliminary chips out of the unformed marble. With the horses the bull was a battering ram, toppling both of them in the course of taking five picks, and consenting meanwhile to become involved in a glorious quite por gaoneras at Calerito's bidding. After two pairs of sticks, he motioned his banderilleros from the ring, dedicated the bull to the children of the Holy House, and closed in with the muleta, stealthy as a bear.

His exordium was a series of statuary passes—passes of death, to give them their ancient name—leading into two groups of hair's-breadth naturals, for which he cited with breast turned bullward and stomach arched fiercely out. There were molinetes to come, and a dozen manoletinas over in the sun, plus some rather vile bits of popular trickery, such as horn stroking and head patting. We chanted *"Ahora!"*—the crowd's intimation that the moment to kill has arrived—and Calerito took our word for it, squinted down the sword and plunged in with icy scientific valor, spread-eagling himself over the horns and burying the blade in the morrillo up to the hilt. The excellent bull swayed to the shelter of the barrera. The gray tongue lolled, the red eyes winked; it slumped, rolled over, kicked, and died. The orphans were delirious with joy. Two ears for Calerito, who strode round the ring like a *louche* mobster from a film directed by Elia Kazan. In 1948, when he was out hunting, his gun went off and killed a member of the Guardia Civil, and to look at him one could conceive it no accident. Someone threw him a live black hen, which he picked up by the legs and slung over his shoulder.

Anticlimax set in with his second bull, a jumpy alarmist whose nerves could not be soothed by either cape or muleta. Calerito's eye let him down at the hour of killing, when he needed three swords and three tries at the descabello. After the second the man behind me started to bark abuse. "I know this Cordoban," he bellowed in my ear, "if his first estocada goes wrong, it takes him till Easter Sunday." I inquired how often he had seen Calerito before. "Never!" he cried, grinning beatifically, breathing alcohol down my neck.

When it comes to killing, a six-footer has a clear advantage over a smaller man; yet bullfighters of Calerito's height are not nearly as common as you would expect. A midget whose eyes are no higher than the horn tips cannot hope to kill with consistent brilliance; yet many of the best modern toreros have been well below average height. Against Manolete and Luis Miguel, the towering exceptions, one can set Belmonte, Chicuelo, Pepe Luis Vázquez, Manolo Vázquez, González and Litri, not to mention the sensation of the 1953–54 seasons, Chicuelo II—all of them stubby manikins. That their lack of inches might be a disqualification seems never to have crossed their minds, nor has it deterred them to know that a Spanish crowd applauds a brave little man no more vehemently than a brave big one. "When the body is small, the heart has to be great." If that is not an Iberian proverb, it ought to be.

The sixth and last fight was, as in most ferias, a novillada, and it provided the meatiest afternoon of bulls we had seen. It is the error of newcomers to disdain novilladas, which frequently arouse much greater excitement than formal corridas. In recent years this has been even truer than it used to be. The apogee of a fighter's fame is often reached while he is still technically a novillero, young enough to take the fantastic risks which time and slowing reflexes have forbidden to older swordsmen. Nowadays the amount of money a matador can make is largely determined by his showing as a novice with junior bulls. In 1949 Spain was afire with *Litrismo* for Litri, in 1954 with *Chamaquismo* for Chamaco; in 1952 four boys parceled out public acclamation between them— Pedrés and Jumillano, who habitually fought together, Antonio Chenel *Antoñete* and the debutant from Venezuela, César Girón. The last two were on the program at Pamplona, together with a lesser name, Alfredo Peñalver; all three were making their first appearance in the town. Girón struck an especially persuasive note. He had lately received a bad goring at Barcelona, and entered the ring at Pamplona wearing a bandage round his head and a fixed wince expressive of stifled suffering. At twenty, he was the oldest of the trio; Peñalver was three years, Antoñete two years his junior. All of them (particularly Girón, whose features are eroded as if by a skin disease) looked much older. No career ages the eyes more swiftly than bullfighting.

Peñalver, who affects a brush cut and grins too much, showed himself a workmanlike fighter; but, though he cut an ear in his second bull, it was plain that dullness of temperament and lack of any attribute which could be labeled magisterial would keep him always out of the front rank. Antoñete, on the other hand, in spite of the fact that he went earless away from Pamplona, stamped his quality on everything he did. He set a hallmark even upon trifles, such as the way in which he swung his cape, testing it before the bull's entrance; every pass was a clue, on which the imagination could build the perfect faena which lurked pre-existent in Antoñete's mind, awaiting only a good bull to bring it forth. So mastery announces itself, by the timbre of its knock on the door.

It is unsafe to assert, as many amateur psychiatrists have asserted, that infantile restraints are responsible for the submerged aggressions which find their outlet in the profession of killing bulls; but it is undeniable that many of the most sensuous bullfighters—Litri and Ordóñez among them—have that in their demeanor which suggests mothers' boys stolidly proving their virility. Antoñete has this overmothered, Fauntleroyal look. He is slim and pliable as a willow rod, surly and contemplative about the face, and capable, one suspects, of considerable private petulance: his mouth has to work hard not to appear weak and sly. Yet he fights with singular honesty and strength—tensed, perhaps, by the task of demolishing the father figure? He was unable to shine in his first bull, which was foolishly underpunished by order of the president, who withdrew the horses after one very light prick. The banderillas were badly placed, and when the faena began the bull was almost untouched and completely unwinded, ready for years more life. Antoñete bit his lip, feeling his way with some low chopping passes, down on one knee, but the horns were far too high for close fighting. He gave up and killed with honorable promptness, to sympathetic applause.

He made sure of his second enemy, however; it was well picked, and in the quites we saw the majesty of his verónica, than which there are few lovelier sights in modern bullfighting. Suave and detached, he regulates the animal's pace without extinguishing its energy: one has seen Furtwängler do the same service to Beethoven. Taking the muleta, he slowed the tempo down still further; this was *legato* bullfighting, conducted in long, circular naturals *en redondo* and easy-pacing manoletinas. Nothing he did was hurried, no flicker of passion disturbed his face. The shock came at the inception of his twenty-fifth pass, when the bull, resentful of the torpor into which it was being lulled, roused itself and stabbed sulkily at Antoñete's leg. He was tossed, and the horn shoved him several yards across the sand. Lacking a slipper but still impassive, he rose and at once prepared to kill. It was the wrong moment. His concentration had evaporated, and he killed faultily, forfeiting the ear which should certainly have been his.

If Antoñete is a torero of the mind, César Girón is a torero of the nerves. He deals in agony. No matter what the cost in grace or dignity, he will stay close to the bull; there he is in his element, with the horns tearing the braid from his thighs and the blood from the morrillo staining his stomach. His disposition is mercurial, and his fights reflect his moods, which may swing from joy to despair in the course of a single afternoon. Two years later he returned to Pamplona as a full matador in a corrida of Bohórquez bulls; with his first he had an ecstatic ears-and-tail triumph, and with his second a disgrace worse than anyone present could remember. One aviso was blown, and still he could not kill; then another sounded, whereat Girón threw away his sword and turned to the president, weeping and pleading that the bull be removed, confessing his incompetence to all who would listen. His appeal was ignored. The statutory two minutes had to elapse before the last aviso ended the farce. The steers took the bull away to be put out of its misery; and Girón collapsed, still deep in his.

Happily, nothing so excessive happened at the novillada. For

Girón, it was a relatively untroubled afternoon; his temper seldom rose higher than frenzy. Looking dramatically lame, he put two nimble pairs of banderillas in his first bull, and then, his eyes darting all manner of nameless threats, snatched the muleta and pranced out to investigate the chances of death at close quarters. The ensuing game of hide-and-seek with mortal injury acted on my nervous system like a slate pencil's scream on my eardrums. He seemed happy in his work; within a minute he was covered in blood, and the more vulnerable parts of his embroidery had been satisfactorily ripped. A series of excellent passes en redondo hinted briefly that there was art as well as anguish in his talent, but when he took the sword, melodrama reasserted itself. Baring his teeth, as if eaten up with passion, he delivered a frankly defective estocada which, by a freak of luck, dropped the bull like a stone. He was given an ear, which, so vulpine did he look, one almost expected him to eat.

In the second bull, to my great relief, the emotional temperature fell below boiling point, and Girón deployed his tricks and tempests to something like tragic purpose. The bull was the biggest and most unpredictable of the day (it weighed 537 pounds stripped), and he handled it with consummate intelligence and knowledge of querencias, by which are meant those parts of the ring where the bull irrationally feels safest and is consequently most dangerous. With the cape Girón was hysterically fearless, above all in a number of passes de frente por detrás—i.e., back to front, holding the cape behind him and presenting his spine instead of his stomach to the bull. Then two pairs of sticks: in these expert hands the run up to the bull recalled a falcon swooping on its prey. And a faena of enormous animation and variety, punctuated with arrogant chest passes which really lived up to the name,

instead of being, as so often and so timidly, elbow passes. A spate
of naturals, beautifully adjusted, to and fro, back and forth, was
interrupted by a sudden goring: the horn cut Girón's ankle open.
But, being one who revives at the sight of blood, he continued,
not limping at all, and finished the series, which he crowned with
a chest pass as flamboyant as a starlet's autograph. The bull toppled
after the second sword thrust, and Girón ran like a rabbit for
cover. But the crowd was already upon him, carrying him shoulder
high, and the applause was breaking like a great wave, when the
last bull of the feast gave up his ears, his tail, and his life to
San Fermín.

The bulls were dead, and the men had survived: nothing un-
toward had disturbed the pattern. For this harmony it was only
right that we should give thanks to Our Lady of Hope, the lus-
trous Virgin of the Macarena, who protects bullfighters and
whose image, blazing with gold, gazes down on the altar of a
drab little church in the slums of Seville. Half a mile away is the
monumental tomb of Joselito, who died in her care. She has a
patient face, full of pity, and two tears are running down her cheeks.

The final junketings took place that night; I must have shared
in more than fifty wine skins. The fireworks were busy above—
first the rockets, worming up to drop down chandeliers, and then
the ear-splitting *tracas*. "Remind you of Guadalcanal, Mac?" said
a voice from Pittsburgh. The erudite shoeblack in the square
made me a present of his favorite book, *See Lass of See Mohicans*,
and the little boy whose father sold paintings dragged me off for
an hour to meet the concierge of the bullring, a cosy middle-aged
woman who looked something like Barry Fitzgerald. She showed
me the bullring infirmary. It was like purgatory, only cold, with

smooth antiseptic tiles, and every door opening onto a minute operating theater, bristling with unfamiliar instruments. "If the horn should have splintered," she said, and held up to my eyes something which I took to be a thumbscrew. Later I was in the square again, clutching a pair of Domecq horns she had given me. I saw a headline in the local paper, congratulating the townspeople on having kept up the traditional gaiety of the fiesta without recourse to undue amounts of alcohol. The paper was folded across the face of a man asleep in a gutter.

Most of the tourists were leaving. Two of the few Englishmen climbed into their car. "Nice fellow, the old *patron*," one was saying, "speaks no English, but his wife's very civilized." It was getting cold: "The town"—I thought of the guidebook—"is not just neat but in addition aerated." A last plate of fried shrimps, a jug of *sangría*, iced red wine with sliced lemons and soda water, and then farewell to the other little boy, with the harelip, who knew everybody: Spain is full of omniscient children. The carpenters were taking down the barriers in the streets where the bulls had run, and the movement of the crowd had changed: dispersing, looking for rest, not converging any more. The shoeblack nodded a brisk good-by—like Litri, I thought, who always nods nervously when the fans applaud, as if he had just obeyed a ghastly command. I walked home past a poster I had missed before; it showed a blue monkey, a camel, and two girls, smiling in knee breeches and top hats. "Formidable Attraction of the Fiesta: the Great American Circus presents with emotion the Great Russian Cossacks." And now that, too, was over, packed up and gone. Pamplona started to sleep, as bulls seem to sleep when life has bled out of them and they lie on the sand. A wind rose.

4

Madrid Interlude

ONE goes to Madrid not to look but to listen; the eye, once pacified by the Prado, can rest without loss behind sunglasses. The modern part of the city, which is most of it, acts as a mart rather than a Mecca for tourism; here you bathe and shave, make reservations, buy clothes for the south, eat lavishly, and call for the English-speaking doctor, who restores intestinal friction with a dark, gritty porridge. Madrid is a city perpetually under construction, where housing developments refuse to develop and planning schemes plot their own frustration. From the amount of scaffolding, and the number of deserted cement mixers and piles of abandoned bricks, you would think its suburbs were peripatetic, their destinies in the hands of men paid to keep them, stone by stone, in motion. At head height all is clean, bright plateau air, but dust ambles around the ankles. Busy, official, social, and sensual, Madrid has never had time to become a showplace. Instead, it is a sounding board for the noisy, fatiguing variety of Spanish conversation, which devotes itself to what William Styron, the novelist, has described as a writer's five main preoccupations: Love Requited, Love Unrequited, Death, Insult, and Hilarity.

I had a week to spare before the Valencian fair began, and two novilladas to see, one in the Madrid ring of Las Ventas, and the

other sixty miles away at Segovia, where the cartel was to include
Pedrés and Jumillano, the young lions of the season. Meanwhile I
eavesdropped, most fruitfully on the foreign aficionados in the
bar of the Palace Hotel. Multilingual bull talk may be heard here
any time from March to September, but the climax is reached in
May, when Madrid celebrates the feria of San Isidro. Then, alive
with an almost proprietary zeal, the French contingent arrives,
sallow and learned, taking its tauromachy very seriously and insisting on the use of classical bullfight terminology in all discussions.
The corrida has, after all, penetrated as far north as Bordeaux;
it is gaining ground all the time, and French bullfight critics,
secure in the terrible finality of utterance to which their tongue
lends itself, write with a frankness seldom achieved by their more
partial Spanish colleagues. Occasionally an English aficionado
breaks through the currency barrier and goes to the fights, wrestling
spasmodically with his sense of shame and his love of horses,
items of psychological luggage which seem overwhelmingly important after a bad corrida, and irrelevant after a good one. But
for every Englishman there are fifty Americans with bull fever;
it is too often our habit, as it is rarely theirs, to condemn things
unseen. A visit to a bullfight is an emotional experiment which
the English fear to risk. The Americans, surprised legatees of
that store of energy and elasticity which has been moving mysteri-
ously westward ever since the heyday of Greek civilization, have
no such qualms. They accept and embrace the bullfight, some
for the right reasons, others because it can all too easily be absorbed,
along with big-game hunting and whaling, into the curious religion
of toughness, and others again because it is expensive and spectacular to photograph.

There are the rich and retired, with a metabolism attuned to manzanilla and elaborate mid-Atlantic accents ("Litri's a tarny little chap, practically a midget, but such artistry! If he were British you'd have narded him by now!"); there are college girls on the Grand Tour who saw one bullfight in France and canceled their reservations in Rome in order to follow the bulls south; there are picaresque vagabonds spending dollars which they earned on the construction of airfields in North Africa; and there are employees of the predominantly bull-mad United States consulates. All are enthusiasts, exhausting themselves by the effort of wanting the fights to be good: "I saw Vázquez last month, and, my God, you talk about guts? Here's what I say to anybody who tries to tell me it's cruel. Just get in there with those bulls, if you love them so damn much. Just get in there. And brother . . ."

A common tableau is that in which a young, crew-cut novice tries out his afición on an older expatriate, whose smudged-ocher eyeballs and rusty complexion tell of long addiction to the Spanish way of life. The acolyte has been explaining, with broad gestures and head-shakes expressive of rueful wonder, his admiration for the valor of Pedrés—"And then he got it, right in the gut, and so help me he got right back on his feet and went through with the kill—" The older man nods wisely: "Yeah, I heard he was good that afternoon. Trouble with that boy, he'll never learn how to coast. Just won't take it easy. I've told him a million times, 'Relax, baby, relax': but no, he's got this Spanish pride and he stays as tensed-up as a watch spring."

"You know him, huh?"

"Know him?" A huge commiserating grin. "Why, we've broken bread with the guy, haven't we, Daisy?"

Daisy is his wife, startlingly pretty with dark hair in a bun. Looking nervously up from the Paris *Herald Tribune*, she supports the half truth: "Sure—sure we have."

After all, they arrived at the party only a matter of seconds after Pedrés left.

"Pedrés," continues her husband, with pedagogic emphasis on the second syllable, "P'drace is my boy, kind of a protégé of mine. Carlos Arruza and I went up this tienta in Salamanca two winters ago, and there was this skinny little kid, shaking in his shoes and looking like a breath of wind'd knock him over. Well, I took one good look at him and I said to Carlos, 'I know what you're thinking, but you're wrong. The kid's got what it takes.' Well, Carlos kidded me for a while—Carlos is a great kidder—but sure enough when P'drace got out there with the muleta, that crowd simply went crazy."

"I saw Arruza in Mexico," says crew-cut. "You known him long?"

"Honey, Arruza"—pronounced Arootza—"Arootza and me are like this. Carlos would cut off his right arm for me. And as for Daisy—why, the guy is just wild about her, do anything for her, isn't that so, Daisy?"

And Daisy, remembering a polite handshake in an airport waiting room, wishfully agrees.

Snobbism of this sort is the occupational disease of the foreign aficionado. Not to have attended a tienta, the trial of young fighting cows which takes place on the ranches during the winter and early spring, is a fearful stigma, almost as bad as not having run before the bulls at Pamplona. Since the death of Manolete at Linares in 1947, there is little cachet in claiming to have known him; everybody does it, from Orson Welles (who actually did know him) to the cloakroom attendant at any Madrid café. A sciolistic acquaintance with a few great nineteenth-century names—Mazzantini, Lagartijo,

Frascuelo—is *de rigueur*; and to have known someone who was in the Madrid arena when Granero was mortally gored in 1922 is practically compulsory. Of matadors living but retired, some degree of familiarity with Belmonte and Rafael El Gallo is essential, and it is advisable to refer to Belmonte by his nickname "Terremoto," which means earthquake. It is no longer fashionable to describe the bull-fight as "basically a religious ritual." "A kind of balletic hunt," is the preferred expression. One should also observe from time to time that the fiesta brava is in decay, that Manolete ruined it, and that nobody has killed recibiendo since 1925. The aficionado's preparation, *mutatis mutandis*, is curiously similar to that of the drama critic.

The study of bullfighting is all niceties, fine technical points which the English language must struggle to convey, and the number of English-speaking authorities is necessarily small. Hemingway, in spite of an absence from Spain which lasted from the civil war to the summer of 1953, thereby denying him access to the thrones of Manolete and Luis Miguel, is among the few who combine passion with genuine knowledge; a tauriform titan with a schoolboy's enthusiasms, a prefect's prejudices, and a games master's geniality. Another real devotee is John Marks, the author of that fine handbook *To the Bullfight*, whose appearance, pouchy and reposeful, puts one in mind of the Rembrandt self-portrait in the Prado with the whiskers shaved off. Crustily holding court at a café on the Gran Via, Marks has the manner of a Spanish bull critic off to perfection, speaking of contemporary toreros as of a gang of unruly children whose caprices may be tolerated and condoned but never mistaken for absolute virtues. It is Marks's misfortune to have acquired an unchallengeable expertise on a subject about which his compatriots are profoundly incurious. But neither he nor Hemingway can com-

pete in length of service with an indomitable and (I swear) non-
fictional Englishwoman whom I will call Lady Black.

Lady Black saw her first bullfight shortly after the armistice of
1918, and afición instantly took possession of her soul. No woman
for half measures, she determined to spread the word abroad and,
backing up her imperfect Spanish with all the tenacious optimism
of Pont Street, assembled three inexpensive matadors, their pro-
testing cuadrillas and a small herd of groggy bulls. These she transported, with a display of organizing ability which would have done
credit to Hannibal, across the south of France into Italy, where they
arrived by train in the summer of 1923. Overwhelming local authorities with her title, her rhetoric, and her refusal to be discouraged,
she succeeded in presenting twenty-seven slightly ragged bullfights
in the velodromes of Turin, Milan, Bologna, and Naples. Understandably elated, she laid plans to repeat the expedition a year later,
only to be foiled by unyielding opposition from the Roman Catholic
Church, which, though it expressed no objection to the impaling of
bulls, took the view that fighting them was tantamount to commit-
ting suicide and ought therefore to be prohibited. This attitude
must have worried some of the troupe, fearful for their souls, but it
had no effect whatever on Lady Black, whose empire-building fore-
bears had taught her to display nothing but amused indifference
when faced with hostile tribal tabus.

Her caravan was already approaching the Italian frontier when
the velodrome proprietors canceled their contracts. Rather than
retreat, she continued defiantly eastward, passing with her bulls,
horses, and men straight through northern Italy to the Balkans. The
men, whose morale she describes as splendid, were nevertheless
becoming difficult to discipline; some of them, in spite of her
expostulations, firmly regarded the entire safari as an elaborate game

in which no holds were barred, and every time the train pulled into a station there were playful attempts to disgorge a bull or two into the midst of the crowds on the platform. By keeping her wits about her and bribing the mutineers with money and wine, Lady Black managed to escort her party as far as Budapest, where it disembarked, blind drunk, in the early autumn of 1924. Sensing that no time was to be lost if it was to be prevented from running amuck, she at once took a short lease on an athletics stadium just outside the city. Here, magnificently, she held six formal corridas of bulls, over which she presided, a Junoesque Madam Chairman with a fan rendered prettily redundant by the icy east wind. The Hungarian audiences, she says, took to bullfighting "like ducks to water," and the fits of mystified acclamation with which they greeted each pass ring still in her ears.

Her mission accomplished, she received from the mayor what may have been either a decoration or a small fingerbowl, and returned to England for the grouse season. She left the railway tickets for her band of tourist executioners in the care of the senior matador, but it was many weeks before they made use of them. Some, indeed, never came back to Spain; the hospitality of Hungarian hostesses is a byword in the Balkans, and to Lady Black, contentedly banging away in her shooting box, there filtered through disquieting rumors about chandeliers smashed, duels fought, and homes wrecked by her impetuous lads. Swallowing her qualms, she sent kind messages of disbelief to her informants, begging them not to repeat idle gossip. The experience however, must have shaken her, for she has revisited Hungary never, and Spain seldom. Since the civil war she has banished herself from the bulls completely, but her afición still burns. You may still meet her at small parties in Kensington, to which, on occasion, she brings her guitar; and, with any luck, as the night wears on, nostalgia will sweep over her and she will sing, in an ululation throaty but sweet, as much as she can remember of the flamenco chants which beguiled that terrible train journey thirty years ago. The idea of a bullfight on ice, which I once propounded to her, did not strike her as in the least bizarre. She is a marvelous woman.

The Madrid novillada was held on Thursday, which thus took on the familiar shape of a bullfight day—a slow, tedious parabola mounting to the fight, and a precipitate slump after it. Abstract thought is an impossibility on bullfight days: two questions rap hard on the mind: whether the rain will hold off, and whether the wind will drop. At five, restlessly, one joins the honking queue of cars lining the Calle de Alcalá, which leads out to the bullring; the pavements are already full of fast-walking crowds, the men predominantly in blue, that electric-bilious shade which is the trademark of cheap Spanish tailoring, and the women pouter-pigeoned in black and crested with mantillas. Though the air is febrile, the streets are not as jammed as they would be for a football match. Spanish *futbolistas* easily outnumber the aficionados; the two largest bullrings in Spain, that of Las Ventas in Madrid and the Monumental in Barcelona, hold respectively 23,000 and 20,000 spectators, who would look like gnat rain on a wedding cake if spread out on the stands of an international football stadium.

The seats at Las Ventas rise steeply from the sand, giving to the place an intent, focused look which is somehow reflected in the audience. This is the cathedral of tauromachy, the end of the pilgrimage; here the matador's visa to glory must finally be stamped; and there is none of Pamplona's tipsiness or Valencia's partisanship. The fight I saw, a minor affair, was nonetheless conducted in a spectral, concentrated hush. A special pathos attaches to the effort of novilleros to prove themselves; I remembered the agony of José Gutiérrez Somoza, who made his debut in a fight at Zamora in April, 1947, displaying such terror and incompetence that he was taken to prison and fined 3,000 pesetas for cheating the public. After a disaster like that, unless one is gifted with the unearthly aplomb of a Cagancho or a Luis Procuna, one cannot live easily. Cagancho and Procuna brush off their disgraces with a shrug, but Gutiérrez Somoza, having once been seen naked and shaking, concluded that he did not wish to be seen anywhere again, and on June 26th of the same year committed suicide.

None of the three novilleros cut an ear, but none of them disgraced himself; the fight was taut and exciting, largely because of the contrast between Navarrito, a Sevillian boy with the sober style of Ronda, and Joselito Torres, a Venezuelan with all the venturesome lightness of Seville. It is, of course, an anachronism to speak of Seville and Ronda as "schools" of bullfighting; Ronda has not produced a torero of much quality since Niño de la Palma, and today there are more madrileño bullfighters than sevillanos. Even so, the terms have their uses, as convenient abbreviations, and that is why they persist. The third fighter was Fernando Jiménez, Manolo González's cousin, moderately brave, but irremediably clumsy with the muleta; and the Yagüe bulls had, as one journalist wrote afterward, "*poca casta y no mucha carne*"—little breeding and not much meat. What gave the afternoon its dignity was the spectacle of Navarrito and Torres controlling their nerves, steadying their bodies to let opposed traditions speak through their youth. The line of his limbs and the strength of his wrist are all a matador has with which to set a signature on his work; and the signature must not offend decorum with its floridity. As Orson Welles puts it, each passing of the bull must announce "not who *I* am, but what *we* are."

Navarrito,wearing a black armband in memory of his father, who had died a few days before, was tall and possessed drooping, waxen eyelids like those of a saint in effigy. With his first bull, a cowardly and short-winded little brute, he declared himself: a poker-faced but passionate dominator. His opening verónicas were admonitions to the bull's vivacity, schoolmaster's passes, and when Torres danced in with some cheeky chicuelinas during the picking, it was as if a child had thumbed his nose while the teacher's back was turned. Navarrito scowled loftily, and the scowl deepened when he saw that the bull was cheating him of his faena by refusing to take the picks. Nor would more than two of the banderillas stay in place: had the creature rubber withers? Navarrito, giving nothing away of his rage, unfurled the muleta and began with four slow, cerebal naturals which must have astonished the bull; in the same state of entranced lethargy he shifted to the right hand, patiently instructing the animal to stay on course. After repeating both series of passes he seemed certain of an ear, but ruined his chances with a bad, nervous kill.

His second bull was a menace, an irrational, high-chopping pick-hater which his technique was not good enough to master; imagine Clyde Beatty given ten minutes to teach a man-eating tiger to jump through hoops, and you have some idea of Navarrito's problem. His peons loyally mimed extreme fright, vaulting in and out of the ring at the least provocation to indicate to the crowd how anxious they were for their employer's safety, but it was no use: Navarrito was baffled. Nothing beautiful could be done with the creature: this was bullfighting as an English audience might enjoy it, an approximately equal contest in which man and bull looked equally stupid, and I

38.

Marin

TEMERITY OF LUIS MIGUEL DOMINGUÍN

Cartier-Bresson

39.

40. A close derechazo by Calerito

41. Another close derechazo by Pedrés

42. Litri's characteristic derechazo, staring at the crowd

43. Litri on his own (note the discarded muleta)

44. Litri

GOING IN TO KILL

45. Calerito

46. Manolo González

47. Rafael Ortega at Valencia

48. A fine estocada by Isidro Marín

49. A moment later. The bull has turned, trampling the matador. Luis Miguel (right), and Marín's peons run in to the rescue.

hated it as much as Navarrito did. He killed, furiously, in great peril, at the second thrust.

Little Torres likewise lost heart with his second bull, a vague perambulator; he yelled shrilly at it like a man hailing a passing cab, but failed to attract and hold its attention. Embellishment, not domination, is his forte, as he had already shown in his first bull, by far the best of the afternoon; a ready charger of which he took advantage to the extent of six impudent verónicas and a sweeping farol, threatening to submerge himself in the folds of the cape like a Boy Scout beneath a collapsed tent in a storm. The picadors and banderillos did their work admirably, and for a moment Torres stood in their shadow, Gulliver in Brobdingnag; then, jauntily, he sprang out with the muleta and easily roused the olés. Bullfighting achieves its proper beauty only when the rhythm of the contest transcends its danger, when you are lulled by the fighter's skill into forgetfulness of the risks he is taking. Of this beauty Torres is not old enough to be capable: a swift, agile stylist, he is effective in fragments but worlds away from Navarrito's sinister, compelling sloth. Citing square-shouldered, he gave us naturals and then passes en redondo, followed by high derechazos and a couple of ill-timed desplantes; the whole faena being chancy, disorganized, and much applauded.

"Il ne leur importe," said Samuel Sorbière, a French visitor to London in 1667, of English theatergoers, "que ce soit un pot-pourri, parce qu'ils n'en regardent, disent-ils, qu'une partie après l'autre, sans se soucier du total." This is equally true of modern bullfight audiences, and it is getting truer every season; the longest cheers go to the pot-pourri experts, such as Pedrés or Chicuelo II, who specialize in disconnected bursts of emotion, rather than to the careful, progressive craftsmen who match their methods to the bull and, working within a strictly limited area, impose on the faena a total shape which stays in the mind after individual passes have faded.

Yet Torres's whirlwind improvisations were what the public wanted. This kind of modern bullfighting—which is four-fifths of it—might be described as classical bullfighting reflected in a smashed mirror. It would not be too much to say that the ideal bullfighter is one who puts into practice the Stoic tenet of *apatheia* as Lionel Trilling defines it: "The principled refusal to experience more emotion than is forced upon one, the rejection of sensibility as a danger to the integrity of the self." In the persistence of their appeal to and dependence on sensibility, toreros of Pedrés's sort become the sentimentalists of the bullring. Intent on fraying our nerves, they debauch our vision. A perfect faena imprints on the consciousness a pattern almost abstract, the pattern of Senecan Stoicism as one finds it in the last act of a tragedy, when the hero stares death in the eyes, and conquers it through indifference. Your Stoic *in extremis* does not exclaim: "See how terribly I am threatened! See what risks I am running! It will be a miracle if I survive!" He says, in effect: "There is no terror. I run no risk that is not of my choosing. I shall survive." This is the statement made by a good bullfighter on his best form, the affirmation that one goes to the bullring to hear.

After a corrida, as Jimmy Durante says in another context, food becomes secondary. It was half past midnight, late even for Spain, before I dined, my companion being an American script writer who revealed that he shared my own bewitched admiration for the English menus so thoughtfully provided by many Spanish restaurants. He cited a wine list in Barcelona which offered "Xeres from Sherry of the Frontier." I replied with a *trouvaille* from San

Sebastian. It had begun, quietly enough, with "Several Kinds of Shells" and "Calamary in His Own Ink"—*calamares en su tinta.* Then, suddenly, the mystery sprang upon one: "Anahogs in a Seamanlike Manner." I never discovered what these were, and did not dare to ask, lest they should be brought (or led) snarling and clanking and hornpiping to the table. I carry at the back of my mind an image of an anahog, feral and shipshape, which comes saluting into my dreams, disrupting every banquet my subconscious prepares for me. Perhaps this was a vestigial anahog, a corruption of an earlier "anchovy" which the scribe, in his ignorance, had confused: I do not know, and it would take a textual critic to find out. At all events, the San Sebastian translator kept up a high standard throughout, ending with a notable flourish on:

Fruits of the Season
Tart of the House.

I am not sure, though, that I do not prefer the *carte* gleaned by my friend in Santander, which included a frugal "Ham with Pea," some pleasantly homely "Cow-Chops," and the macabre recommendation, as *spécialité de la maison,* of "Toadstool Omelette."

We discussed the novillada at length, went on to the style of the Sevillian fantastics in general, and then, by what seemed a natural progression, found ourselves talking about Chaplin. I had noticed this happening before, in many other conversations. There is an undoubted kinship between the tidy skippings of the fastidious little tramp, his alertness in avoiding disaster by ducking under a beefy arm or sliding down a drain pipe, and the equally slick maneuvers of Sevillian toreros eluding the horns. What W. C. Fields said of Chaplin has been echoed by many American aficionados speaking of Manolo Vázquez: "The guy's a goddamn ballet dancer." In both cases the man exposes himself, in a spirited, volatile, balletic manner, to all kinds of danger, and emerges unhurt. The quiet, withdrawn Ronda style has nothing of this: there is philosophy in it, something more august and profoundly moral than the practical, life-loving shrug of the Sevillians. With the *rondeño* fighter the bull takes on a majesty it seldom achieves with a Sevillian, to whom it is merely a threat to be skirted as glibly and neatly as human reflexes will permit. Hence tragedy belongs to Ronda, because tragedy is not, as a rule, animated or vivacious but still and reflective. Ronda is imaginative and classical; Seville is fanciful and baroque. The distinction is much the same as that which can be drawn between *cante hondo*, the pure form of Andalusian song, and *cante flamenco*, its more popular derivative.

The Sevillian (not Hemingway's horse) is the true comedian of the bullfight. His pre-eminent quality is not so much courage as pluck; he charms rather than binds a spell. He reminds one, not too distantly, of the clown bullfighters who somersault baggy-trousered over the horns of *becerros* in the arc-lit circus spectacles which invade many bullrings during fiesta weeks, nocturnal parodies of the afternoon's serious business. And here we are back once more at Chaplin, for comic bullfights, known as *charlotadas*, were invented in direct imitation of his early one-reelers. The first and greatest of the Chaplinesque toreros was Carmelo Tusquellas "Charlot," who made his debut as a burlesque matador, complete with bowler, cane, mustache, and high-buttoned frock coat, in Barcelona on May 8, 1916; his success was immediate, and the impresario Eduardo Pagés at once formed a full comic cuadrilla.

In addition to Charlot, he engaged Rafael Dutrus "Llapisera," already well known as a taurine *farceur*. Llapisera's trick was to enter the ring clad in flawless evening dress with what Cossío, the historian of bullfighting, describes as "all the seriousness of an English humorist." The combination of Llapisera and Charlot (who must have resembled Keaton and Chaplin) proved irresistible, and the team was and is widely mimicked. So that in linking Chaplin with bullfighting I am merely repeating what Pagés intuitively spotted nearly forty years ago. In his celerity, his serio-comic delicacy when matched with a mighty Mephistophelean bruiser, Chaplin behaves much as a *torero sevillano* behaves in the presence of a bull. We laugh at Chaplin because the peril is artificial; the bullfighter, on the other hand, may be killed before our eyes. Though one smiles at Sevillian antics, one is always conscious that one's amusement is a form of *Galgenhumor*.

It is appropriate that Chaplin's most celebrated party turn, never seen on the screen, should be an impersonation of a nervy matador. And it is equally revealing when a recent biographer, Robert Payne, quotes him as saying of the tramp character he originated: "I am always aware that Charlie is playing with death. He plays with it, mocks it, thumbs his nose at it, but it is always there. He is aware of death at every moment of his existence."

Another actor who uses a Sevillian approach to drama is Jean-Louis Barrault, a brilliant mime, tumbler, talker, and thinker whose stage presence is nevertheless without real weight. He and Chaplin have much more in common with each other and the bullfight than they have with, say, Olivier in the great days of his *Oedipus Rex*. For a hint of the ideal *rondeño* actor, one must go to John Gielgud, whose style is surgical in its detachment, nobly removed from the tumult; like Manolete, he has a way of sadly averting his head, as if something malodorous offended him, whenever the character he is playing is beset by danger, death, or the loss of a job. And though he lacks Manolete's baleful compassion, he shares with him the knowledge that he is a cynosure, on which the impressionable will model their ideals of human dignity. Gielgud's remoteness, his commanding poise are the marks of the swordsmen of Ronda. Their pride, that of men able to dominate through the mind rather than the muscles, informs and vivifies all he does.

Toughness, it should by now be clear, is no part of a bull-fighter's equipment; many of the best have been tubercular or syphilitic. No aggressively masculine skills are required for the job; indeed, if a torero's work declares too blatantly his gender, it often militates against the best of which he is capable, as if a painter were to assert that he was a man first, and an artist second. This is not to say that there are more homosexuals in bullfighting than in any other profession involving self-exhibition. It is simply to suggest that interpretative art, particularly in such a stylized form as the bullfight, does not depend on our awareness of the executant's sex. Universality is aided by ambiguity. We laugh at a comedian when he exposes the feminine traits which lie beneath the masculine appearance; when Bob Hope, having bragged of his fearlessness, screams at the sight of a mouse; when Jack Benny broods about crowsfeet and thinning hair; when Sid Field dons his velvet coat and transforms himself into a fairy-legged photographer. Chaplin, especially in his early films, is the arch effeminate of comedy: observe the bashful hunching of the shoulders and the girlish grin with which he accepts an unexpected compliment, and notice how, in *The Cure*, he squirms with coyness when constrained to undress in the men's changing room. In all acting where finesse is uppermost, there is a female spring in the mechanism; and this is true of the bullfight since Belmonte developed it from a hunt into a form of self-expression.

Anyone whose business is the study of human behavior in a crisis—and this of course includes actors—can learn a great deal from the corrida. Ristori once nettled Coquelin by declaring that to simulate an emotion it was necessary for an actor to have experienced it; to which Coquelin replied: "Yes, madame—but I have often seen you die!" thus ending the dispute. Myself, I think Ristori was in error, for I have seen too many actors "feeling" an emotion so intensely that they were quite unable to communicate it; but I believe she might have answered Coquelin's point if she had remembered the bullfight. At the climax of a good faena, you know precisely how a man looks and behaves and, with cognate clarity, something of what he feels and thinks in the presence of death. An actor might play Cyrano better for having seen Cagancho in the ring, alternating comic high jinks with tragic pride, and anyone contemplating Mio in Maxwell Anderson's *Winterset* and wondering how to cope with the death-shrouded last act would be well advised to watch Litri facing a Murube bull. When you have seen that, you know a little about dying.

5

Segovia

SUNDAY's fight at Segovia was to be a novillada of high prestige. The bulls were announced as Cobaledas, though on the eve of the fight they fell ill and had to be replaced by animals from the lesser-known ganaderia of Muriel, and the fighters were the summer's three musketeers, Juan Montero, Pedrés, and Jumillano. This would be Jumillano's last appearance as a novillero in the neighborhood of the capital; on August 12 he was to take his alternativa at Barcelona. The English and American colonies were formulating heated little plans for making the journey, sharing each other's cars, cadging lifts, reselling unwanted tickets at "exactly what I paid for them—only twenty per cent over the official price." The press was sure to turn up en masse, because Pedrés had signed a contract a few days before with Litri's agent, the ex-matador Camará, who handles none but the most phenomenal of phenomena.

A deep mistrust of rubble-spattered Spanish roads and wine-flown English drivers moved me to take the train to Segovia. Halfway there, a sudden hailstorm sent knobs of ice as big as knuckles clattering down onto the starved Castilian plain, and I had a twinge of aficionado Angst: a black cloud on bullfight day is as bad as a burst blood vessel. But the sky was soon wiped blue,

128

and I spent the rest of the trip quarreling with an English-speaking Spaniard, who maintained that the bullfight was barbarous, though he had seen only one, and that a good one, in which eight ears were cut. Though I protested, I could not help seeing his point, against which there is no fool-proof argument. There will always be those to whom the thought of a bullfight is *per se* repellent, like an unopened book whose contents are reputed to be pornographic. No matter how hard such people try to keep their eyes impartial, prejudice betrays them; the obscenity leaps out from the page, vile and glaring, and even if their deeper judgment pronounces it not obscenity at all but an essential detail of a great design, they will ever afterward think of the volume as a dirty book, and themselves as slightly contaminated by contact with it. The censor in one's mind is as capricious and twice as inconsistent as the Lord Chamberlain, and his power is absolute.

All the same, I should quake to see him evicted, and the bullfight held to be a pansy pursuit, which is what Nero or Caligula would have thought it. Reading Suetonius's gossip about the midnight games in which Nero, dressed in a lionskin, would roar through the arena savaging the flesh of tethered slaves, I try to isolate the qualities which make this revolting and the bullfight acceptable. Both involve bloodshed; both are intended to enliven an audience; and both are exhibitions of fundamentally needless cruelty. In both cases, pain is publicly inflicted, and no apologist for the bullfight, however strong his convictions, could reasonably offer as a moral justification the excuse that animals feel pain less intensely than human beings.

I have no respect for the aficionado who fails to argue the matter out with himself, though I have to admit I do not know the solution. Must one go to the awful length of saying that, in the

case of the bullfight, the end justifies the means? Which implies
agreement with the view of Ximenes, that the unification of
Spanish worship justified the Inquisition: a hard doctrine for most
of us. When all the debating points have been made, I am still
unable to reconcile the logical reasons for loathing the corrida,
which are as logical as the reasons for loathing horror camps or
the building of the pyramids, with my own obstinate awareness
that it represents for me a summit of human aspiration.

On two questions, however, the dispute on the train helped me
to make up my mind. My opponent scoffed at the notion that
bullfighting was an art; and at bottom, though I offered a token
shriek of scorn, I found myself of his opinion. It is not an art in
itself, but the cause that art is in other men—poets, for example,
painters, sculptors, and musicians. The matador is not, by any
definition that pretends to strictness, an artist any more than
Beowulf or Odysseus were artists; like them he is an epic adven-
turer in whose deeds there is enormous incidental beauty, whose
life is the raw material for an unwritten narrative poem, a *Belmon-
tiad* or *Litriad* in embryo.

Shifting his fire, the Spaniard next insinuated that there was a
strong element of sexuality in bullfighting, a line of argument
so naïve that I almost asked him how much sexuality he thought
there was in the annual rifle championships at Bisley. Nobody
denies that Nero's cannibal frolicking had a specific sexual purpose; and it is certainly possible to read sexual symbolism into
the events of a bullfight—I know a girl whose psychiatrist told
her that the bull represented her mother and the matador her
father, adding that she herself was the horse. But it is nonsense
to hold that algolagnia, sexual pleasure in the infliction of pain,

plays any part in the ritual; the corrida is never, in the ordinary sense, sadistic.

On the other hand, in another, more precise sense of the word, it is sublimely, even exultantly sadistic. Mr. Geoffrey Gorer has defined de Sade's general philosophy as one of "pleasure in the ego's modification of the external world." This pleasure can—and in de Sade's case did—lead to indulgence in pyromania and kindred fantasies; but it is present, less antisocially, in most of us. And nothing satisfies it better than a man demonstrating his mastery over a force as objective and uncompromising as a fighting bull. Some of us, finding nobility in the spectacle, can accordingly cite as our text: "The admiration of the noble draws us upwards." Others, finding nothing there but self-indulgence, turn away in horror and all efforts to convert them are wasted. The question of bullfighting probes spots so sore that for the aficionado Jowett's advice is perhaps the best. Never apologize, never explain.

The fight more than made up for the squalor of the journey, and for the blistering walk, along a road turned into a dust storm by Renaults and Cadillacs, from the taxiless railway station to the bullring, a shallow structure raised up a few hundred yards away from the Roman aqueduct. For a pagan festival, what more fitting cincture than the baked striation of Segovia's Roman walls? Outside the ring a mob prospered, selling drinks, peanuts, shrimps, eyeshades, chocolate; inside another mob sweltered, giving off a volume of noise and a variety of smells which made concentration on jasmine, silence, and swimming pools difficult but imperative. Country bullrings combine the greatest discomfort with the smallest chance of escape; even for fatalists, they are a considerable strain. The heads of the crowds were packed together like cobbles in a street, and all were perspiring. The word SOMBRA on my ticket was somebody's dreadful joke, it being quite clear that the sun would continue to fry everyone present until at least two bulls had been disposed of. One sat, meanwhile, on what felt like the rim of an active volcano.

Segovia did not run to *alguaciles*, the mounted heralds who customarily lead the procession; instead, a midget equestrienne performed, delighting us for far too long before the paseo struck out across the lumpy, hillocky sand. Pedrés and Montero walked on either side of the lanky Jumillano, whom alone of the trio I had seen before. He is sort of emaciated *jeune premier*, who wears an expression at once dazed and sickened, which one attributes to long off-stage minutes spent straining to achieve relaxation. The year before he had been a laughingstock, grade A meat for the bulls, learning his trade by a good deal of trial and as much error, getting tossed at least four times in every fight; this year, the publicity said, he was the greatest, most emotional and crowd-storming torero in Spain. We would see. On his right was Pedrés, looking sour and sensitive, and on his left the chunky Montero, whose lopsided face and solid build suggested nothing so much as the ex-prizefighter Eric Boon.

Montero plainly has a genius for taking punishment, and that afternoon he needed it; given half a chance the crowd would have lynched him. I discounted the howls of abuse which went up every time his picador so much as made a move in the bull's direction; rustic crowds are quite English in their detestation of the picks. Nor could I blame Montero for dispatching his first bull, a leaping manso, almost unplayed. But there was no excuse for his second faena. The deliberate quenching of a willing animal is always a depressing sight, and when it is combined with failure to complete a single pass and total incompetence with the sword, the effect is emetic.

When a matador thrusts the sword in a few inches and withdraws it without letting go the pommel, it is called a *metisaca*. On his showing at Segovia, Montero's mastery of the *metisaca* is not likely to be rivaled in our time. After his first abortive stab he decided, in an ecstasy of foolishness, that the bull's head was now low enough to receive the descabello, a decision which is best left to veterans of the stamp of Antonio Bienvenida and which, ten minutes later, he was bitterly regretting. Anticipating the first aviso by seconds, the bull died, as much from fatigue as from anything else, and was removed from the ring to the better-run slaughterhouse outside.

What I am about to write will serve as an illustration of the pitfalls inherent in all bullfight criticism. My impression of Pedrés, based on his performance that afternoon, is as accurate as I can make it, yet it will probably be unrecognizable to anyone who has seen him since. Bullfighting confounds prophecy by never, in any circumstances, running to form; it demands of the fighter so delicate a balance of aptitudes that the slightest disturbance can send them sliding. A good torero can turn overnight into a caricature of himself, the responsibility for which may lie with a family bereavement, an inflated bank balance, a sexual disappointment, a horn in the thigh, or a cold in the head. Or any of a hundred other irritants. I cannot say which, if any, of them has afflicted Pedrés since he became a full matador. Nor am I particularly curious to know. Whatever has changed him has eviscerated him, stripped him of authority in the ring; but it cannot alter the fact of what he was, for a few memorable afternoons in the summer of which I am writing. And that at Segovia merits some kind of tribute.

He shared with Litri that privacy which goes by the name of public solitude; his glamour, if he had any, was that of the hermit. Many bullfighters carry to an extreme the practice of living in the moment, extracting from each lost second its last ounce of panache: but Pedrés went deeper. You would have said he had a sense of history and knew that, although perfection was not to be sought in his lifetime, it was something to be built toward, and the knowledge passed on to other initiates. His manner of playing the bull gave the onlooker the sensation of watching a secret experiment, one of an infinite series being performed by an anchorite working under sealed orders. Such was the depth of his concentration that he seemed to suspend time. He was then eighteen years old, dark-haired and sallow-featured, with two deep furrows between his eyebrows. K-Hito, the critic of *Digame*, did not exaggerate when he called Pedrés "the most philosophic of contemporary Stoics."

With the cape, as he showed in his first bull, he was extremely maladroit; Jumillano's interventions in quites were infinitely better, in spite of their gawky splayfootedness. The cape is not Pedrés weapon any more than a machete is a surgeon's. Nor was his first faena notably good; he began with the customary derechazos, with naturals ensuing, but the bull, like the forever-to-be-cursed Bailador which killed Joselito, had a defect of eyesight which forbade it to see clearly at close quarters. Pedrés's method of coping with this fault was, to say the least, idiosyncratic: instead of citing from a distance, he moved in contemplatively and cited from within a yard of the horns, where he and the muleta appeared to the bull a joint indistinguishable blur. He neither smiled nor looked at the crowd; only at the bull; and the bull looked only at him.

Late in the faena he ventured on his own pass, the pedresina, which is a more exposed version of the dosantina invented in 1949 by the Portuguese torero Manuel dos Santos. Pedrés has evolved a number of closely related passes, all of which turn on the presentation of his spinal column to the bull. For the pedresina he takes the muleta in his left hand and peers back over his right shoulder at the bull; when the charge comes, he turns his head to the left, watching the horns over his left shoulder as they slash past his hips. On this occasion the bull blundered too close and knocked him off balance, making him look as stupid as only an inventor can look when his invention blows up in his face. After a well-judged kill he was granted an ear, but threw it away, disgusted by his failure to do better.

A single glance told him that the second bull allotted to him, a frisky gray, was the right size and speed for his technique to work on; one guessed, too, that its horns, short and branching inward, were unlikely to inconvenience him. After one pick and two pairs of banderillas he appealed to the president, montera in hand, to have the acts changed. I should explain, parenthetically, that the business of act changing is not nearly as clear-cut as it sounds; the bullfight is too fluid to be chopped into sharp, separate parts. The preliminary capework is still going on when the trumpet blows for the horses to enter; the horses are still in the ring when it blows again for the banderillas; and the dedication of the bull which precedes the faena is carried out with peons fussing in the background, placing the bull in position for the matador to start work with the muleta. The gray came to Pedrés full of vivacity. Testing its honor with two series of naturals, still as a sunflower on a windless day, he found it frank and noble; and at once proceeded to lead it into his private labyrinth.

As he solves the odd problems he sets himself, Pedrés reverses much of accepted bullfighting technique. He defies the ancient theory of terrains; instead of fighting with his back to the barrera, he repeatedly sets himself between the bull and the *afueras*, the arena in the center of the ring which is the bull's natural domain and toward which it naturally veers at the end of a pass. What is more, he multiplies the risk implicit in this positioning by adopting it for the execution of the tricky rearward passes he loves. He is not ignorant of terrains; it is simply that he chooses to flout them. In this he is a revolutionary, and, unlike most revolutionaries, he does not appear to be standing on his head merely to disguise the fact that he suffers from foot rot. He can, when he wishes, give you a chest pass which would be the envy of Julio Aparicio, and his skill in changing the muleta at speed from right hand to left is exemplary. With the gray bull his serpentine back-to-front style paid remarkable dividends of emotion: the angles and tangents of his mental blueprint became plastic reality. "Us professors," blustered Jimmy Durante when his new car broke down, "don't get out of the lavatory too often"; but the result of Pedrés's calculations needed no such excuse. They were novel, but they worked. After a single estocada, the bull fell and the experiment was over; finding the president's estimate in agreement with his own, Pedrés impassively accepted the award of both ears, and harshly rebuked one of his peons who prematurely cut the tail. It had been a fascinating and original performance; and the bitter truth is that Pedrés never afterward improved on it. The old maxim still holds good: in art, new departures do not always lead to new arrivals.

Emilio Ortuño Jumillano is a prodigy of a different order: in Pedrés's background, a poor family of Albacete, there is no bullfighting blood, whereas Jumillano's father is a popular and respected impresario. Few boys can ever have worked harder to live up to a parental dream. Jumillano, so lean and elongated that he seems to have been carried to the ring from the rack, is all effort, all corkscrewing and gyration. The flimsiness of his build is such that when he shrugs his shoulders they appear to be shrugging him. Even the cape drags him earthward under its weight, causing him to sway like a poplar in a hurricane at every verónica. One thinks of Caesar's:

> This common body,
> Like to a vagabond flag upon the stream,
> Goes to and back, lackeying the varying tide,
> To rot itself with motion . . .

His walk is a long-legged, bestilted shuffle, like that of a clockwork doll; he wobbles from side to side, and I am under the impression that he has flat feet. Added to all this, he wears an unhappy squint, which seldom leaves his face while he is fighting.

In the bullfight, as in the playhouse, the *optique du théâtre* makes inexorable demands, and Jumillano's physical awkwardness is so oppressive that he will never become a national idol. Yet of his courage there are no doubts; this ramshackle junior Quixote works incredibly close to the horns, and one nearly always ends up admiring him. Nature cast him as slender, and life summoned him to play Hamlet. With his first bull he failed, wherefore he steeled himself to make us gasp with his second. Bad luck again: it was a bland, backward weakling. Undeterred by a swinging, hacking pair of horns, he embarked on two series of naturals, finely intended but ruinously ugly in execution. By now he was quite prepared to get himself impaled to the toril gate if it would stir us; so he waddled (tall as he is, waddle is what he does) close to the horns, edging his hips nearer an inch at a time, and cited for a dosantina—once successfully, but at the second attempt his pants were ripped. They gave him an ear, which he knew to be no more than a courtesy.

With our rib cages cracking under the pressure of the crowd, we rose to leave: and then sat down again, for the fight was not over. Furious with himself, Jumillano had decided that this should not be the last bull he would fight as a novillero before a Madrid audience; and accordingly he exercised his right to call for the *sobrero*, the substitute bull which awaits in the corrals in case one of its fellows is rejected. This is an expensive decision to make; even a novillo can cost something like $570, and if a torero chooses to fight an extra bull he must pay for it himself. But nothing would now prevent Jumillano from putting personal honor before the family fortune, and within seconds the encore had begun. Pedrés and Montero had already left the plaza with their squads, and Jumillano's picadors were on the way to their hotel. He cajoled and commanded the seventh bull, a magic black, in such majestic fashion that it brought tears to my eyes, and he did it without a single pick and with only one pair of banderillas to damage the creature's sheen. K-Hito wrote next day: "Emilio, who will enter the university of tauromachy on August 12, took his entrance examination yesterday at Segovia. The result: a scholarship!"

His veronicas were marvels of concentration, and all his cape-work was good, but it was with the muleta that he left the deepest marks on my memory. He dedicated the bull to the public, and then made it a present of the most electrifying dosantina I have ever seen, the one he had failed to complete with the previous bull. He did it in *tablas*, with his back to the bull and the sword-pricked muleta in his right hand, taking the horns across his kidneys so slowly that you could hear them brushing against the braid. *Valse mélancolique et langoureux vertige*; the solemn rhythm of the pass sent Baudelaire's line surging into the mouth, and the body surging up from its seat. Jumillano was now keyed up for adventure, and the rest of his faena was the purest war poetry, a bodying-forth of the emotion contained in Olivier's delivery of "Once more into the breach . . ." Lonely and gangling five minutes before, aspiration had transformed him; he had become our ambassador to the court of death. In ten fluent naturals he examined the possibilities of self-destruction, leaning over so far as he followed the passes through that he looked like a human croquet hoop, yet such was the power of that monarch bull that the absurdity of the pose escaped us. Strength flowed from the tableau they made together, in passes ancient and modern, wise and foolish, common and rare. And all the time the man was advancing, flinching no more than his enemy, whose mouth was bravely closed throughout. In the middle of the ring, the heart of the enemy's kingdom, Jumillano met the bull's wish on his sword, seeming to swivel on the horns as the blade drove in.

With the death of the bull, the ring burst from its trance into life; coats, shoes, hats, two cameras, and a pair of binoculars sailed down; we stood and sobbed, and the Americans behind us were sobbing too; they who had shrieked, "You bastard!" at every picador in Spain had now seen a perfect bull ideally fought with no picking at all; the slate was wiped clean. The attendants, in a delirium of butchery, hacked off the ears, the tail and two hoofs for Jumillano; thus encumbered, he was hoisted shoulder high and whirled twice round the arena. He threw the tail to the man on my right, who kissed it and stuffed it into his breast pocket, from which it dangled as he cheered, like an obscene handkerchief.

The journey home to Madrid, on a crowded, stinking, unlit train, was a riot of harmony, an international congress gone mad with good fellowship. Everyone had been to the fight, and Jumillano's triumph bound us all together, Spaniards, Englishmen, Americans, Frenchmen, Portuguese, and a hairy, astounded pair of Finns. We were as free and as elated as if we, and not our hero, had gone through the place of death into the sunlight. I was drenched with spilt wine when we pulled into Madrid, just after midnight. Dinner on a café terrace with five total strangers, one of whom gave me his shoes; the trees silent in the garden below, and the trains buffeting in the distance; gazpacho, the stinging cold soup of the south, metallic Spanish champagne, and paella sticky with lobster and oil—these are the signals for a picture to light up in my mind, whose theme is the annealing warmth that follows a good afternoon with the bulls. A part of the picture shows Jumillano, laughing as he was carried round the ring and saying: "Is that it? Is that what you wanted?"; and in another, darker corner is Varelito, who also spoke to the crowd as he was borne from its presence to his death in May, 1922. "This is what you wanted," he said through his agony. "This is what you wanted, and I've got it. Now you can be happy."

6

Valencia: Part One

IN POPULATION Valencia is only the third city of Spain, but in afición it is second to none. And what an afición! Not the feckless, frantic dilettantism of Pamplona; not the judicial augustness of Madrid; but a fierce partisanship which splits households, stirs up street fights, and is wholly in league with chaos. Valencian afición is rapturous, exasperated, and pitiless, and it can blow hot and cold overnight: witness the icy blast it directed at a local torero named Chaves, to whom, after a few bad performances, a public urinal was dedicated. Granero was born in Valencia, and if his reputation is still high in the town, that is because he had the wit to get himself killed before it languished. Litri's mother came from Gandia, thirty miles down the coast, and though her husband lived in Huelva, she returned to her birthplace to bear his son, whom the Valencian public has treated ever since as its exclusive property, to be harried and cosseted, loved and reviled according to whim. It was in Valencia that Litri took his alternativa, and from that moment the savage bear hug of the town's adulation never loosened its grip on him. The tendency when I arrived was to despise him, to dismember him ritually, failing by failing: and as Fritz Haarmann, the Hanover werewolf, said of his own homicidal orgies: "*Man macht das leichter, wenn man liebt.*"

Having temporarily given up its belief in *litrismo*, Valencia had turned *dominguista* for the season; the toasts in the cafés were all to Luis Miguel; and in spite of the technical arguments advanced by the local bull strategists to explain this baffling change of temper, one suspected that they had decided to like Luis Miguel principally because Madrid loathed him.* At the periphery of all such debates, hissing execrations, there stood the city's licensed heretic, a furtive, forty-year-old journalist named Vicente, who would declare on the least provocation that to set Litri against Dominguín was to set a flea against a louse and that in his view the virtue had gone out of bullfighting with the retirement of Domingo Ortega.

Vicente, who wears a gray raincoat, has a gray face and conveys the impression that there is a bomb in his pocket, is a professional repository of bullfighting rumors. Today's corrida, he whispers, gesticulating with an ash-laden cigarette, is doomed as usual, because as usual the bull's horns have been clipped and shaved down. Bullfighting does not lend itself to the commoner forms of corruption, in that nobody could conceivably be paid to lie down or to throw a fight; but horn shaving undoubtedly existed for those who could afford it until the protest made in the late autumn of 1952 by the matador Antonio Bienvenida, who issued a statement to the newspapers which at once ventilated the abuse and gained the reformer a good deal of welcome publicity. A bull which has had two inches filed off its horns and the tips sandpapered down has lost not only its power of daggerlike penetration but also its ability to gauge distances: since it cannot see its own horns, it is likely to miss its target by a vital two-inch margin. As a result of Bienvenida's charges, an old regulation, long-neglected, has been reinforced, and nowadays

* Perhaps the final comment on Luis Miguel's unpopularity was made in 1954 by his friend Ordóñez. "Who is right," a reporter asked him, "Luis Miguel or the public?" "The bull," said Antonio.

the armory of every dead bull is examined by a veterinary surgeon as soon as it has been dragged out of the ring.

But for every ill that is redressed, happy malcontents like Vicente can point to a dozen that flourish unhindered. His talk is full of bulls stunned with sandbags to weaken them, bulls pricked with novocaine to deaden them, bulls lamed by having their hoofs clipped, bulls dizzied by being transported upside down in their boxes, bulls bred specifically to destroy themselves under the pick, bulls chilled in cold water to slow them down. Fear of reprisals, he mutters, prevents him from giving documentary evidence to support his fantasies, some of which may be outlandishly true. He comports himself like a man on the run, even when he is sitting at a café, and he says that the toreros fear him because he writes the truth about them. I recommended to his attention a Madrid magazine called *El Burladero* (which has since expired), as being the only publication I knew which printed frankly critical accounts of bullfights; most of the others are subsidized directly by bribes and indirectly by full-page advertisements which are paid for by the matadors' agents and may be withdrawn if their clients receive unfriendly notices. I knew Vicente well enough not to be surprised when he replied that he had founded *El Burladero* in the thirties, and that the present editors were fraudulent impostors who must some day be exposed and jailed.

After each bullfight in Valencia, idle crowds follow Vicente, monkish in his battered black suit, to a street corner near the bull-ring. Climbing up a wavering stepladder, he chalks his impressions of the fight on a blackboard fixed outside a jeweler's shop. Alongside the board are three framed indicators, each provided with an arrow which he manipulates so that it points to *"Colosal," "Muy Bien," "Bien," "Regular," "Mediocre," "Mal,"* or *"Desastroso,"* according to his opinion of each torero's performance. The chalked comments themselves reveal much about the Spanish tradition of decorum in print; when Vicente is being, as he thinks, heroically outspoken, he uses language which an American dramatic critic would take to mean scarcely qualified approval. His mission of iconoclasm accomplished, Vicente slouches off, defiantly puffing a Philip Morris, to a neighboring café, there to drink *horchata* and to await stoning as his reward for having told the truth about—say—Luis Miguel. What he has written will generally be: "Today the great lawgiver of the fiesta broke one or two of his own magnificent rules. He was less than perfect, and his work with the sword, though marvelous, was not historic."

Vicente is the Spanish nonconformist who has almost forgotten how not to conform. Even his caricatures (he is a pen-and-ink artist too) verge subtly on flattery. All the same, he enjoys his role, relishes the narrowing of the eyes and the tightening of the jowl which precede with him the confidential communication of some screaming platitude. He seems always about to pounce, but his claws are not as sharp as he thinks they are.

Palmerston, among others, remarked that life would be endurable if it were not for its pleasures, and Valencia *en fête* bears him out. Normally a cramped and fetid industrial town, low-lying and somewhat malarial, enlivened only by trams and shipyard clamor, it is transformed twice a year into a madhouse; once in the spring for the pyromaniacal feast of Las Fallas, and again in July for the feast of San Jaime. These celebrations are twice as deafening as those at Pamplona; the firework factories which dot the province are kept at a fever pitch of inventiveness by the rival demands of a score of fiestas up and down the coast, each vying with its neighbor in the amount of damage it can do to human eyes and eardrums. Valencia emphasizes fireworks, not only by night but at noon: bright bombardments which threaten to split the sky. Strings of crackers are hung along the squares, and if you turn your head for a moment someone will drop a squib in your coffee. After a few hours of Valencian gaiety, you feel capable of catnapping inside the brass drum during a military parade. Though the bullring is next door to the railway station, it is a crypt by comparison with the uproar in the streets.

We began with an appetizing novillada, stating the theme for the crescendo of corridas which lay ahead. The cartel was Antoñete, Jumillano, and César Girón, whose previous appearance in Valencia had been much publicized and had ended in confusion. As at Pamplona, Antoñete made his quietness eloquent; his first faena was a classic of youth, of controlled ardor and humorless grace. One of the patent limitations of the bullfight is that it can never be tender; and a witty faena is almost as rare, though I have seen Arruza attempt it by making each pass a cunning parody, giving us his versions of the naturals of Luis Miguel, Procuna, Armillita, and Manolete, each distinct and hilarious. Antoñete's work with the muleta was stern and fine; again and again we saw the pedigree simplicity of his chest pass, interlarded with a richness of naturals and manoletinas. In a day of good killing, he emerged the maestro, and plainly qualified for the title which the French critics had bestowed on Manolo Vázquez the year before: *le grand petit torero.* He took an ear from the first of Atanasio Fernández's novillos, and two from the fourth, in which he showed a finesse of management astonishing in such a stripling. This was a tricky bull, with a horn-spread so wide that neither Jumillano nor Girón liked to enter its territory. Antoñete took it into the sun and let it play with him in naturals, ayudados, and dosantinas; but eagerness begat carelessness, his recurrent fault, and he was tossed and trampled. Like a tongue of flame from matchwood, he sprang up and killed with a demolishing estocada.

He was everywhere that afternoon, popping up discreetly to steal all thunders: he took the edge off Jumillano's first bull by intervening in a quite with an exquisite *mariposa*, Marcial Lalanda's butterfly pass, wherein the torero holds the cape behind his back with both hands, swinging it from side to side as he moves gently backward. Nothing could be more dangerous, for if he should lose his footing the bull is upon him in a flash. Jumillano failed to repeat his triumph at Segovia: he went through a scrappy faena with a drowsy animal, which he killed inopportunely through the lung.

These were, on the whole, superb little bulls, stout and eager and direct, with strength and sleekness equally commingled: as striking, in their miniature way, as the celebrated Fermin Bohórquez sextet which went to the San Isidro fair at Madrid in 1954. César Girón drew the best pair. The first was an ugly duckling, since it had almost no tail, and something of a rudesby, since it sang incessantly, but its valor was preposterous. Girón took it untouched through a flurry of chicuelinas, and then saw it send horse and picador somersaulting over its horns, upon which Antoñete darted in, flushed with excitement, to administer a wild, whooping serpentina, that catherine wheel of the cape, and a svelte pass de frente por detrás. A misplaced pick damaged the animal's rib cage, and I felt my dreams of a fine faena crumbling; but Girón was bent on giving us our money's worth, first with three pairs of sticks and then with a faena hectic to the point of morbidity. Not once did the muleta leave his left hand; we saw a series of thirty variations on the classic natural, interspersed with two complete redondos which took the bull in U-turns round the torero's motionless trunk. Two ears for the Venezuelan.

The entrance of the last bull, high horned and looking for trouble, brought the crowd up cheering and insisting that the breeder rise in his seat, which he did, to acknowledge their gratitude. The battle with the horses was formidable. Twice the picador was unseated; and twice he was propelled across the whole diameter of the ring by the dash of the bull's onslaught. I have seldom seen a bull state its majesty with so little equivocation. The five picks it took might have been flea bites. Girón licked his fingers and seized the sticks: it was a time for virtuosity, and brilliantly he provided it, with one pair *al cuarteo*, another *de poder a poder*, and a third in the perilous manner known as *al quiebro*, for which the torero, having drawn the bull's charge, holds his ground, and feints to right or left with one foot, thereby diverting the animal from its course and enabling the man to place the sticks as the horns pass his hips. This was loudly cheered, and the faena could be nothing but anticlimax. The bull had learned too rapidly, and was anticipating Girón's every move. His naturals were not coming off; in desperation he resorted to adornos, manoletinas on his knees, every melodramatic device he knew, but it was useless. The fight was ebbing away from him. Out of self-pity he began to limp, dramatizing himself in the character of a hurt child deprived of its place in the sun; and still the bull went for him and not for the lure, like Kipling's "Bull That Thought," which pursued "the person, not the propaganda: the proprietor, not the journal." He had some compensation, after a bad kill, when the fans swept him and Antoñete shoulder high from the ring. There were conquerors in the streets of Valencia; and Vicente clambered up his stepladder, moved Girón's arrow round

to "Colosal," and laboriously chalked: "The Venezuelan invader
has returned: and at last his Atomic Bomb has exploded!"

The beach which serves Valencia is situated in the suburb of
Grau. To reach it you grind for two miles on a squalid little tram
through tattered slums, past bleached warehouses and dockyards,
loud with the clank of riveting and shaking in the heat like the
picture on a badly adjusted television screen. The sand, when at
last you tread it, is an evil gray. Apart from the Restaurante Pepica,
where the mussels served with garlic and tomato are as good as
any to be found between Barcelona and Málaga, the rows of eating
shacks lining the *plage* are fly-blown and uncomely. Yet, lunching
there next day, I wished myself nowhere else in the world. I was
in the company of aficionados, and a corrida was imminent. The
bulls were from Samuel Flores, and the swords would be in the
hands of Luis Miguel, Rafael Ortega, and Ordóñez, who was making
his first appearance as full matador in the Valencian ring. He had
spent most of the season outshining Litri; and he had chosen
Valencia as the climax of his campaign. Within twenty-four hours
Litri would be in town to meet the challenge.

The cartels had been so arranged that the two boys would not
fight together until the fifth and last corrida of the fair. This
was not alone a conflict of wills: it was the matching of two con-
tradictory views of bullfighting, the clash of two schools, a
tauromachic civil war. The Taurine Club of Valencia had added
a fillip to the controversy by offering a reward to the matador who
obtained most trophies-per-bull-killed during the week; one point
was to be scored for each ear, tail, or hoof cut, and the total divided
by the number of bulls each man fought. The prize was a golden

ear, and a portrait of the winning matador would be hung in the bullring museum.

There is something cheap and indecent about competitions of this kind; they degrade the bullfight by forcing it to overlap with the race track or the athletics meeting; nevertheless, the rivalry between Litri and Ordóñez had produced an atmosphere so tense that any solution, even one based on numerical calculation, was to be welcomed. There was, of course, Luis Miguel to be reckoned with; and Vázquez was a popular outsider. . . . So we talked, in circular fashion, returning always to Litri and Ordóñez; and the corrida moved nearer, the hour of the *clarín* and the crowd's great shout.

It was Dryden who said, "I hate your Spanish honour, ever since it spoiled our English plays." By which he meant, of course, that inflated, egoistic code of fealty which, in the English tragedies of his day, so often and so dully vied with love in the hero's breast. But in a broader sense Dryden was speaking for England at large. Is not Spanish pundonor, which lures urchins into the ring to outface the bulls, always incomprehensible to the English mind? I believe it is, and grieve that it should be so. The scholars hold that Dryden's contemporaries wrote spectacular plays about pride, death, and honor as a form of escape from the meanness of their age; as Allardyce Nicoll puts it, "heroism in real-life plays would have raised too sharp a distinction between what was and what might have been." For a hundred years after the end of the eighteenth century, the great majority of Englishmen were too puffed with self-regard to notice the cutting edge of that distinction. They allowed the Victorian drama to endow its heroes with impossible constellations of virtues; and nobody thought to complain that life outside the theater was only superficially virtuous and very rarely heroic. All sense of the blatant incongruity between art and reality seemed to have deserted them; or perhaps they saw it, and did not care. In their vanity they identified themselves with the frock-coated stage heroes who performed for them; this was, they felt, the mirror held up to nature.

We cannot feel that today; half a century of spiritual diminution has robbed most of us of our smugness. The ineffable nobility of the Victorian protagonist, which delighted our ancestors by flattering them, delights us in a different way: we laugh aloud at it. We are aware that we are giants no longer, if indeed we ever were; and we are oppressed by the skill with which psychiatry has charted our littleness. We still have a taste for heroism; we weep compassionately when a Channel swimmer is drowned; but heroism allied with beauty we regard as an idealistic fiction. Were it to be presented in a modern play as a fact of everyday life, we would, like the Englishmen of Dryden's day, openly scoff at it. Yet some part of us is hungry for it, anxious to be reassured that it still exists; and that may explain the steady trickle of English and the flowing stream of French visitors to the bullrings of Spain. They go to solace themselves with the contemplation of a rite in which, on a good day, heroism and beauty, the great absentees of Western Europe, may be seen happily and inextricably embraced. In an age of fluid moral codes and relative standards of conduct, Spain stands fixed as a lighthouse, blazing a message of personal honor as she did three centuries ago. The message is independent of politics or religion, and would be much the same if the civil war had ended in a Falangist rout. For others through her religion, for me through her national pastime, Spain continues to justify Keyserling's description: "The moral touchstone of Europe."

Which ought to preface a panegyric of the afternoon's corrida. Unfortunately it cannot. The anticipated splendor was, in Edward Young's phrase, "all darken'd down to naked waste." The main culprit was Luis Miguel, who began to sulk as soon as he saw that the plaza contained one or two rows of empty seats. He took this as a personal insult and a reminder that the only practicing torero whose name on a bill guaranteed "House Full" or "*No Hay Billetes*" was Carlos Arruza. Luis Miguel was irked, and showed it, and not even the quarter-million pesetas he was earning for his afternoon's work could console him.

In their litheness, assurance, and physical versatility Arruza and Luis Miguel are natural competitors. If you set them down in a gymnasium they would promptly engage each other in rope climbing and horse vaulting. For both of them the ordinary suertes of bull-fighting are too easy; they are forever seeking new complications. Luis Miguel has been known to pick a bull which he afterward prepared with the banderillas, fought with the muleta, and killed; and in Mexico Arruza once brought off the incredible feat of killing a bull with the sword in his left hand. Yet for all their stupendous agility (perhaps because of it), neither of them can transmit a spark of emotion. When Kemble played King John, Hazlitt summed up his weakness in a sentence which might have been ready made for Luis Miguel: "The varying tide of passion did not appear to burst from the source of nature in his breast, but to be drawn from a theatrical leaden cistern, and then directed through certain conduit-pipes and artificial channels, to fill the audience with well-regulated and harmless sympathy."

Stephen Potter's Lifemanship has its exponents in bullfighting as everywhere else, and Luis Miguel is their king. He makes fools of his rivals by exposing the tricks of their trade; and in so doing

makes fools of the audience, who begin to regret their enthusiasm
for maneuvers which they now see to be as easy as pie. He is like
one who should explain to a group of children that the story which
so consumed them with its terror and beauty was a mere fictional
invention, cooked up for the money. Scott Fitzgerald somewhere
complains that most of those who abuse Hollywood are at fault
because they cannot see the ventriloquist for the doll, cannot
distinguish between the surface *kitsch* and the complexity of
resourceful techniques behind it. Luis Miguel encourages the
opposite error. With him you can't see the doll for the ventriloquist;
he is showing you how to pull the strings, telling you how the trick
is done. And as he does so, the magic disappears.

One has seen this happen a thousand times in the theater. It
happens, indeed, in most performances of *Othello*: few actors playing Iago can resist the temptation to wink at the audience while
they are leading Othello through the ghastly faena which ends in
his death. "See how easy it is!" they seem to say, at once degrading
Othello and themselves. Luis Miguel has the same ensainted con-
descension, the same habit of performing in front of an invisible
mirror. He is a magnificent all-rounder betrayed by his own
virtuosity.

He had bad luck with his bulls, which were heavy and dull
as buffaloes. His first refused the picks; Luis Miguel, not to be
outdone, refused it the honor of placing the banderillas, whereat
the crowd jeered. He took the sword and muleta and flapped them
dispiritedly under the bull's muzzle. Having shown us that we
could expect nothing from it, he gave us nothing himself, beyond
a quick estocada and a scornful descabello. He was slightly less
perfunctory with his second. The verónicas through which he
lounged were competent, and did not blaspheme against the saint

50. Rafael Ortega, having placed the sword correctly but without killing
the bull, finishes the job with the descabello

51. Luis Miguel and a dying enemy

52. The death. Matador: Manolo Vázquez

Cartier-Bresson

53. Matorell in disgrace after a bad fight

Cartier-Bresson

54. Isidro Marín in triumph

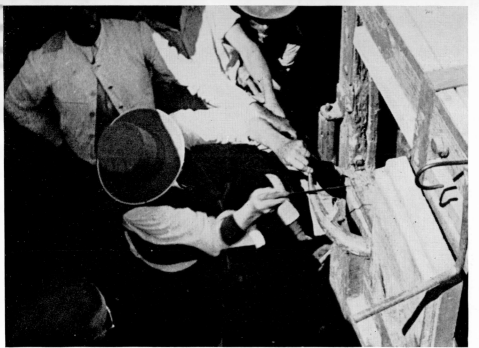

Fineras

55. Horn-shaving (afeitado), a vanished abuse

56. The bull is pent up in a box, its head held in position by a rope. Above: two inches of horn are sawn off. Below: the stump is filed down to the semblance of a point

Fineras

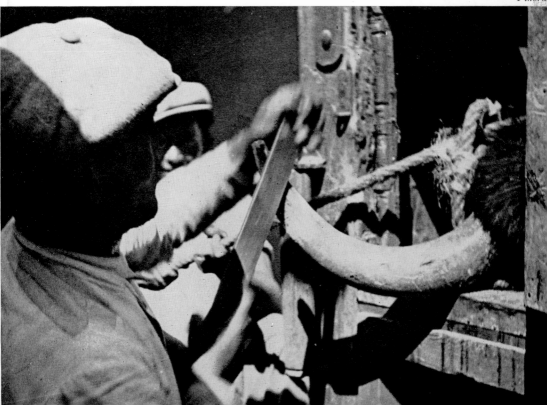

57. Litri with tail and hoof

Luis Vidal

58. Ordóñez with ears and tail

Luis Vidal

**THE LAST FIGHT OF THE
VALENCIAN FAIR, 1952**

Hermes

59. Manolete

60. Calerito dedicates

Peter Buckley

61. New blood: Chicuelo II

Peter Buckley

after whom the pass is named. The two pairs of banderillas which he placed, after an exceptionally crude bout of picking, were admirably neat. But all the time he seemed to be pitying the bull's inadequacy; and pity, as Max Beerbohm has said, is little sister to contempt. He certainly dominated with the cloth, but there is no pleasure to be derived from watching the domination of a corpse. His derachazos were wide and lazy, his naturals tired and without heart. Four afarolados and an adorno, kneeling with his back to the horns, were not enough to restore his credit, and he killed so disgracefully (four thrusts) that one expected him to take the course which legend attributes to Cesare Borgia—that of decapitating the bull.

If this book were being written fifty years ago, and the fighters with whom it deals had been active then, its hero would not be Litri or Ordóñez: the choice would fall inevitably on Rafael Ortega, who took the second and fifth bulls that afternoon. For Ortega's style looks back to the pre-Belmonte era; almost alone in Spain, he deserves the name of matador. He is a born killer, whose work with the sword, resolute and honorable, is the criterion of his art. "The King of the Volapié!" shout his advertisements, and for once they do not exaggerate. The Cordoban Machaquito, who was in his prime around the turn of the century, killed 1042 of the 1853 bulls he fought at the first thrust, and Rafael (not to be confused with Domingo) Ortega is his legitimate successor.

Though he was only twenty-eight years old in 1952, his portly carriage and receding hair made him look much older; you would think he had walked out of one of those nineteenth-century bullfight prints in which the matadors are tree trunks, not saplings. For Ortega la lidia is neither tragic nor comic; it is a job to which he, a professional death dealer, applies himself with tough, stout-hearted honesty. He is gored at regular intervals, and has more than once had the priest at his bedside; but whereas many bull-fighters get wounded in the course of fanciful departures from the rules, Ortega suffers from the austerity with which he attempts to obey them. His conscience has made a pin cushion of him.

He had a strange pair of bulls. The first pelted into sight, sniffed, and leaped the barrera without giving the matter a moment's thought. Foxhunter could not have made a cleaner jump. Bulls have been known to clear the callejón, land in the front row, and carve up the audience: this one was content to rampage through a panicky mob of civil guards, swordhandlers, and pressmen. It cornered a local photographer, sent his apparatus flying and slashed him lightly in the calf before being guided back through an open gate into the ring. Ortega shaped up for one of his square-shouldered, old-fashioned verónicas, but this blundering bull forgot its lines again and gored him, too. Chaos seemed imminent, as when an actor enters drunk through the wrong doorway in the wrong act. Ortega, who had only been grazed, took great pains to give us a sincere and punctilious fight, based on three series of correct and moving naturals. The bull—"like a coal his eyeball"—was roused to some appearance of royalty; Ortega worked close and respectfully; and all went well until the king of the volapié went in to exercise his dominion. A wind blew up, fluttering his muleta and making the bull jumpy, so that Ortega took four stabs before achieving the perfect estocada he had promised himself. Yet so classical was his manner of profiling and entering that each pinchazo was worth a round of applause, the crowd being fully aware that there are easy ways to kill and that Ortega, having chosen the hard way, was miss-ing the mark only by millimeters. All the same, he lost his ear.

In his second bull, loss degenerated into robbery. Ortega braced himself to give of his best, and the bull cheated him, retreating from the muleta and cold-shouldering every blandishment. Five weary minutes passed while Ortega lined it up for the sword, swinging it past him so that it should come to rest parallel with the barrera, steady on its feet, with the front hoofs properly together. The wonderful instinct which told him when to launch his estocada, crossing over the horns and ending the fight in one second of splendor, had forgotten to warn him that by now our attention had wandered. Perfectionism, as Ortega must often have reflected, has its penalties.

It was Ordóñez, of course, who took the day's laurels. Fate sent him, in his first bull, a starring vehicle, hand-made for his gifts, and Valencia rose to him as he gave it ten memorable verónicas, standing tiptoe and angelically calm, without a peer in Andalusia. After that he could scarcely wait for the horses to leave the ring, and when one pair of banderillas had gone in he turned to the president, unable to contain his impatience, and asked for the last act to begin. His wish was granted; and, snatching the muleta, he dived into a rising wave of emotion. Literature offers but one real image of Ordóñez at his best: the boy on the burning deck, whence all but he have fled. Alone in the ring, he is the last survivor; a powder monkey defeating single-handed an ominous and bristling armada. He brings off his victories with supreme insouciance. The right hand is posed, elegantly but firmly, on the hip, lightly clasping the sword hilt, while the left hand draws the fire. After the naturals came a pretty bombardment of passes high and low, rounded off with a slamming estocada. Luis Miguel watched from the barrier, his face an ambiguous deadpan, as Ordóñez took an ear and two circuits of the ring. The applause must have told him that a palace revolution was in process. The court favorite was trying on the crown for size.

Ordóñez failed in his second bull, but that can have been small comfort to Litri, the old pretender, who was fighting the same afternoon at Barcelona, cutting no ears and making no friends. When he arrived in Valencia next day, in one of those ancient upright Hispano-Suizas which bullfighters favor for their luggage capacity, he had much lost ground to make up, and that in a town full of his detractors; he returned as a son, but a prodigal one, for whom there would be no fatted calf until the Valencians had seen a few well-killed bulls.

Outside his hotel, the new Excelsior, a flashy affair with spindly modern furniture and plump pageboys like bottle-green partridges, a gaping crowd had collected. It may be true, as Salvador Dali says, that "the bull is a Spanish god who sacrifices himself; bull-fighters are only his priests": but it is for the fighter that the laurels are plucked and the lynching mobs gather: the priest has undergone an apotheosis. As Litri stepped out of the car, shrugged his suit into place and walked into the hotel lobby, followed by Galápago, his wizened peón de confianza, some in the crowd whistled, and one urchin asked him cockily how he had liked America. The debacle of his Mexican trip the previous winter was maliciously fresh in everyone's memory. From the port of Palos, a few miles from Litri's house in Huelva, Columbus sailed in the summer of 1492, returning eight months later with the fruits of the New World. Litri had returned in shame, bearing only the sourest husks.

It was now July 25. Litri had fought in ten corridas since the beginning of the month, and gained from them only two ears, one at Palma on the 5th and another at La Linea on the 13th. Just ten years before, in the season of 1942, Manolete had come to Valencia under similar suspicions of eclipse, with only two ears on his tally for the month. Within five days he had silenced his critics for good, five days of sustained magnetism in which the slim, aquiline Cordoban reached the height of his powers. The record, a scarcely credible document, deserves reprinting:

July 23, Valencia: Alipio Pérez bulls: four ears and two tails.
July 24, Valencia: Villamarta bulls: two ears, a tail, and two hoofs.
July 25, Barcelona: Galache bulls: two ears, a tail, and a hoof.
July 26, Barcelona: Santa Coloma bulls: four ears and two tails.
July 27, Valencia: Galache bulls: three ears, a tail and a hoof.

Writing of this succession of triumphs in the Madrid press, three critics found themselves invoking the name of Seneca; and in all, about a hundred thousand words of tyrianthine prose, as well as numerous ballads and broadsheets, have been composed around the killing of those ten bulls. Among English-speaking journalists Manolete sometimes fared less happily. His death, five years afterward, was chronicled by an American news magazine in one laconic line: "Died, in Linares, Spain: Manolete, claimed to be world's bullfight champ." Was Nijinsky, then, world's ballet-dancing champ?

Litri's name on the cartel brought the crowds out earlier than usual. While he was still at luncheon, picking at a piece of steamed fish, the narrow streets leading to the bullring were blocked by the afición. A nasal babble of expectation almost drowned the groaning of the trams and the bugle blare of jammed cars. A bottleneck of customers formed at the bullring gates, shoving, expostulating, sweating, and swatting flies, and the roofs of the hotels overlooking the arena were crawling with nonpaying specta- tors. Once inside, we were thrust by mass propulsion past cushion sellers and beer vendors up dank stone steps until the blue circle of sky, guarded by flags, spread out above us. Here we waited, fanning ourselves, nibbling potato crisps, greeting friends, taking slow breaths to quiet the heart's unruly beating.

Nobody paid much attention to González, who took the first of the Galache bulls. The little man gave it half a dozen bad right- handed passes, and then pushed in the sword. The glum prelude was over. It was now time for Litri.

I remembered the last time I had seen him in the Valencian ring. Twelve months before: and he had been gored. The bull, a broad- horned creature, had jolted him to the ground in the middle of a series of naturals; viciously, he beat off the peon who vaulted the barrera to help him, and completed the six passes he had intended. Whisking the muleta over the muzzle, he walked away for his applause, at which point the bull charged, neatly piercing him twice on the inner side of his left thigh. It was a goring full of emotion. I. A. Richards has stated that the effect of poetry must be described in terms of the resolution of opposite impulses. Tragedy, he says, is a balance of two such impulses: pity, the emotional accompaniment of an impulse to approach, and terror, the emotional accompaniment of an impulse to retreat. So it is at a bullfight; and so it was at Litri's goring. Both impulses were there, and in the war between them I was dumbstruck. Looking drained and nacreous, Litri was carried to the infirmary, and Luis Miguel killed his bull for him, while the bats that infest the town began to whisper and scutter in the smoky air.

Next morning I visited Litri's hotel, bearing introductory letters from a school friend of his who had made a thriving business out of writing them. I was wondering whether he would still be unconscious, when he passed me on the stairs. Of course he had recovered, he said, and of course, if God was with him, he would fight again that afternoon. We sat down, I agog with admiration, he staring unwinkingly at his hands, which were clasped between his knees. Talking like a convict, in snatches from the corner of his mouth, he said he did not mind big bulls. "When they are big," he said, "they cannot see me. They take me for an insect. As I fight them, I grow, and that is the pleasure." The brown eyes flashed up at me when I asked if he had any rivalries. None, he said; nor did he admire any one of his colleagues more than the rest: "The public is the judge of fighters. I am just a judge of bulls." That afternoon, with his thigh strapped up and in considerable pain, he passed the death sentence on two Domecq bulls, and deprived both of their ears.

All this was running through my mind as Litri's first bull came into the ring. It was very small indeed, so small that angry men rose in their seats and bellowed for the pigmy to be removed. In the middle of the tumult Litri stepped out and calmed us with six stunning verónicas and four brave gaoneras, the pass, as many people present must have remembered, in which his dead half brother had excelled. Whatever might have leaked out of Litri in the way of enthusiasm and devotion, he remained faithful to his earliest admirers: these regional sympathies, as the present government knows to its cost, are practically indestructible in Spaniards. Valencia stopped grumbling, and waited, hushed, for Litri to take the sword and muleta, the keys to the code language of valor which is his mother tongue. The genius of Spain is a manual affair, a matter of miraculous fingers: snapping in rhythm, flicking at

castanets, stroking guitars, steering brushes over canvas, or guiding
the course of the smooth notched stick from which the red serge
droops.

What followed was a faena of extempore lunacy. Propounding
his general law, Brunetière said: "In drama or farce, what we ask
of the theater is the spectacle of a *will* striving toward a goal and
conscious of the means which it employs." Litri was certainly
striving; but the means he was employing seemed to be out of his
control. All was hasty, disjointed, and inconsequent. Litri behaved
as nervously as if he were on trial for his life in front of a packed
jury. He began with three chest passes, which is like beginning a
poem with three colons. These seemed obscurely to please him, and
he wheeled slowly into six derechazos, keeping the bull as far away
from him as a high-school horse circling the ring at the end of his
trainer's whip. Growing distrait, he ventured upon naturals, after
the second, fourth and sixth of which the bull slipped and fell, a bad
pupil for Litri's dancing class. Suddenly, before you had time to
blink, he caught fire, and summoned the little bull to menace him:
there were seven manoletinas, in which he stared at the sky, and two
more on his knees, the bull having to duck its head to avoid scratch-
ing his armpit. He finished the series without rising, threw away
sword and muleta, and stonily awaited his applause. His spasm of
ardor had exhausted itself; his kill was without distinction; but he
had done enough to deserve an ear. His plea of "Not guilty" had had
its effect, and the crowd postponed judgment.

Manolo Vázquez, who took the third bull, eclipsed him without
effort by emphasizing in his faena all the classical figures of bullfighting which Litri ignores. Everything he did was scented with
Seville, with a beautiful briskness beside which Litri's improvisations looked amateurish. The faeno progressed through statuary

passes to derechazos, long and lovingly followed through, then rose to a peak in naturals; and then, before the kill, declined with deceptive nonchalance into molinetes, as Mozart will sometimes allow us to take breath before racing a symphony home. One estocada cut short the exhibition, and the prize was two ears.

González, out of his depth, exercised his usual arts of ruin and waste. Four ravaging picks set a splendid bull grunting and wavering, sending it into the faena with its nose brushing the sand. Earthquakes would not have moved it, and González could have fed it sugar with impunity. He punished it further with chopping passes until it stood dazed, unable to lift its head. What might have been an enemy had been neutralized into a patient. Was this well done? González seemed to think so, for he was smiling quite happily as he put his victim to death, the crowd meanwhile roaring its resentment.

When the fifth bull plunged into the ring, I was watching Litri, who stood crouched behind the burladero while his peons ran out to make the preliminary tests with the cape. The Galache took the lure, charged, swung, turned, and charged again, straight as an arrow; and Litri took a long, deep breath. This was a master bull, a *toro de bandera*. A small boy in the sun guessed as much, and leaped into the ring, fluttering a home-made muleta on a wooden spoon, but the peons speedily pinioned him and swept him over the barrera into the arms of the police. Almost tripping over his cape in his anxiety, Litri scuttled out to face the bull and, citing properly for once, wrapped it around him in six resplendent verónicas; the technical knowledge which had lain *perdu* for so long rushed out to his fingertips. Folding up the cape, he looked significantly at his picador, El Pimpi, who nodded back and, when the bull charged, thundering into the padding, administered a perfect *vara*, with no twisting or gouging, as if this were the normal run of picking instead of a shining exception. Another followed: horse, bull, and man interlocked in a strong, clean grouping. The banderillas, too, were put in with exemplary precision, three pairs in an area no bigger than a saucer. Litri tightened his lips and shook out the folds of the muleta. First dedicating the bull to Valencia, he showed Valencia the depths of its sin in mistrusting him.

His faena was of an intelligence and complexity beyond all my hopes, and iconoclastic into the bargain, a Vázquez faena turned inside out. As always, he led off with the garnishings instead of the meat: who but Litri would initiate a faena with eight mano-letinas in the center of the ring? As the bull passed, he tipped his flinty little face backward, for all the world like a child successfully imitating his father at a party. A crazy sequence of passes next took shape—afarolados and molinetes madly mixed together—all with unbroken rhythm, and all twenty yards away from the nearest auxiliary. They succeeded each other like images in a symbolist poem, a series of shocks which coalesced into meaning only at the end of the sequence. This was the montage technique applied to bullfighting.

No sooner had the olés died away than Litri changed the muleta to his left hand and moved into a majestic minor key; one after another they flowed, unmistakable for anything but what they were, clear and authoritative naturals in the grand manner. Sounding cheap and tinny, the band struck up a pasodoble; and Litri shouted the traditional challenge, "Whuh-hey! Whuh-hey, toro!" citing for his tenth and last pass in that concord of excellence. What we were seeing was something which is seldom made public: an instinctive artist had stumbled upon a classic form and made it so intimately his own that one would have thought he had invented it. The stresses of his temperament had led him irrevocably toward the form which was waiting to express them, the father of all passes with the muleta, the pure natural with the left hand. The pressure of despair produced the revelation.

Nor was this all. Refreshed by what he had done as by a blood transfusion, Litri now showed us the marvel with which he made his reputation. Away from the bull he ran, turning after thirty yards, and took the muleta in both hands behind his back. The crowd's susurration gave place to an icy calm, across which Litri's voice echoed: "Whuh-hey! Whuh-hey!" He shook the cloth, fixing the bull with his eyes. It sniffed and turned: pondered, twitching its tail. "Whuh-hey!" It started to lumber toward him; after five yards, to canter; and Litri remained nailed to the ground, gazing over the approaching horns at the stands. At twenty yards the charge was a gallop, the bull bounding toward the flickering cloth and the puny, glittering legs steady in front of it. One prophesied disaster; evisceration, without a doubt; but no, the horns were swerving, following the muleta as it swung slowly away from the man to become a separate target. By his art Litri had taught the bull that apart from itself the cloth was the only living creature in the ring; the dancing red serge was the challenge; and the bull took it, letting the man go free. "Tell him not to do that!" begged a man in the callejón, covering his eyes with his hands: Litri has several passionate admirers who follow him everywhere, yet have never dared to look at the conclusion of that pass. "Tell him not to do it again!" But he did it twice more, and killed superbly.

A great clamor arose, the noise of turncoat Valencia changing its mind and welcoming home its adopted son. He was cheered three times round the ring, with two ears in one hand and the tail in the other. I seem to recall that there was a sixth bull, a big one, and that Vázquez, having failed to break its spirit with punishment passes, stabbed it in the neck in a lather of fear; but I would rather not let that drab coda mar the pure song of Litri *redevivus*.

7

Valencia: Part Two

I REMEMBER the fourth corrida—Luis Miguel, Litri, and Vázquez
with bulls of Clemente Tassara—as the occasion of Dorsey Slade's
conversion. Dorsey Slade was an unbalanced American, young,
squarely built, with a face like an intelligent dog, who had just sold
his first novel—250,000 words about his childhood—for publication
in the spring. The publishers' advance, he explained, had been
enough to pay for a trip to Europe; en route for Italy he had seen
a bullfight in Provence, after which nothing would do but he must
pursue the bulls into Spain. He arrived in Valencia a few hours
before the Tassara corrida, when I met him at a café in the Plaza del
Caudillo, grumbling to a small group of his compatriots about the
brutality with which his novel had been cut. He had a New England
accent, lank black hair and a wild laugh, and he spoke thickly,
peppering his conversation with deliberate but charming obscenities.
"Those bandits slashed me to ribbons," he was saying, referring to
his publishers. "Those bastards carved me down to the bone.
They were sharks, Tynan, and I'm not kidding. I gave them half a
million words and they made me shrivel them down into a goddamn novelette."

I gathered that Dorsey had been an international mountaineer
until two years before, when he had broken his leg badly in two
places; out of sheer boredom he had taken to writing, and now

172

bullfighting had restored to his life the element of physical risk which had been lacking in it since his injury. He had begun to see himself as a sort of sawed-off Hemingway; his was a stubbornly *non-raffiné* personality, and he approached bullfighting with his brows knit, passionately determined to be moved to tears. He was equally determined not to be deceived by "phony frills"; Dorsey was an extreme case of that brilliant negative talent which is the distinguishing mark of postwar youth—the ability to see and expose phonyness a mile off, coupled with a maddening inability to do anything constructive about it. You find these joint qualities in the heroes of J. D. Salinger's *The Catcher in the Rye* and Kingsley Amis's *Lucky Jim*, two novels which are prescribed reading for anyone wishing to understand the generation that grew up during the war; and Dorsey Slade might have modeled for both of them. Except that he had escaped, and they had not.

Life for Dorsey had become a *farouche* truancy; he was buccaneering his way across Europe, alternately chortling and sulking, with his shoulders hunched and his hands sunk fathoms deep in his pockets. Withal, his capacity for admiration was unbounded. He admired Salinger and Sherwood Anderson and Dos Passos; and he could admire himself less self-consciously than anyone I have ever known. "You know something, Tynan?" he said, gripping my arm as we rose to leave for the bullring, "I may become a torero. It's on the cards. I'm strong and I'm as brave as hell." I said that strength had very little to do with it. "Trouble is I'm too damned old. And I'm too short to go in over the horns. But I'll tell you about the horns, Tynan: they don't scare me." He was mocking himself now, parodying the Hemingway Neanderthal as he told me about the horns. "I have real muscle," he went on, "and my stomach is exquisite, rippling muscles meeting and crossing. And

I'll tell you a secret," he said, pointing at his navel, "I'm a mass of hair from here on down." He chuckled, and then gripped me again. "So help me," he said, striking himself a painful blow on the chest, "if something pretty happens in that ring today, I'm going to get so sexually hopped-up that I'll get in there and kill the rotten bull myself." Fired by the thought, he whipped off his jacket and executed a precarious verónica alongside the mudguard of a passing car. I remonstrated with him, pointing out that in Spain this was regarded as an insult, since it implied that the driver of the car had horns and was thus a cuckold. "Thanks for the light, Tynan," said Dorsey grimly, wearing what Kingsley Amis would call his brother-in-arms face, "I appreciate that. Keep me in line, I'm a peasant." As we entered the Plaza de Toros, his eyes fell on a bullfight poster depicting a matador halfway through a chest pass. "Look at those buttocks!" he cried. "Poetic!" He bet me fifty thousand francs that he would fight a bull before Halloween, and then prowled off to find his seat.

The weather was menacing. The sky was like dirty sheets, and swags of black cloud roved across it in a high wind. Things could not have been less propitious for the kind of ecstasy Dorsey was bent on experiencing. Bullfighting and cricket have this in common, that they need the sun to spread their wings. A corrida under clouds, unless it is spectacularly good, looks somehow impertinent; the toreros become midgets in fancy dress, wantonly defying the displeasure of nature; and even the least superstitious spectator feels slightly unnerved. Former patrons of the Open Air Theatre in Regent's Park will know something of what I mean.

Luis Miguel in black and silver was wary with the first Tassara, a low-horned rover which hugged the fence. Both with the cape and the muleta he issued his familiar invitation to the waltz, but the bull politely declined, even when Luis Miguel came closer and offered to dance cheek to cheek. The faena was a stammering contest, with the bull chopping and halting and the man bored and hesitant. He managed a few naturals and some glib dosantinas, and then killed at considerable length. There followed the extraordinary affair of the second bull, Litri's bull.

Imagine a public square alive with bands and banners for the ceremonial unveiling of a statue, every circumstance ripe for a great occasion; and imagine the trumpets sounding, the veil dropping, and the statue immediately crumbling to dust. That was roughly what happened to the second bull. It came out bursting with bravura, showing immense dignity as well as terrifying powers of acceleration. Litri ran straight out to the center of the ring and got a huge ovation for six commanding verónicas; spurred to further temerity, he went on to a trio of chicuelinas, each more experimental than the last, for this is a pass Litri has never mastered. Vázquez replaced him with the cape and gave us, as a sort of corrective footnote, one perfect verónica and one flawless chicuelina, and Luis Miguel plumped down on his knees for three flashing faroles.

A sense of mastery was in the air. What we were watching had the force of a fine play: the bull was the protagonist, the constant factor, and the interwoven triple plot of the three matadors, each coming to terms with the enemy in his own way, made up the action. After the capework with that second bull the analogies between the bullfight and dramatic convention struck me more vigorously than ever. The Aristotelean definition of tragedy, as interpreted by Francis Fergusson in *The Idea of a Theatre*, fits bullfighting like a glove. The action, the "thing to be done," toward which all subsidiary motives tend, is "to rule the bull, with valour and beauty." Every member of the *dramatis personae* is involved in the active verb, "to rule," and subordinates himself to it. The prologue, the "thing given," is the bull's entrance; the *agones*, or explorations of conflicting purposes, are the capework of the three matadors. This overlaps with the *peripeteia*, the reversal of fortunes, in which the bull, hitherto the master, becomes the victim of the picks and banderillas. The faena leads into the epiphany—the "ultimate vision of the truth" toward which the action has been moving.

Litri, poor wretch, never reached the epiphany, largely because there was no reversal of fortunes. The picks and sticks missed their marks, and the bull came to judgment in complete control of the ring. The plaza trumpeter announced the faena with a prolonged fanfare in arpeggios, which must have chilled Litri's marrow, since he knew he could not live up to it. He started classically, with six statuaries close to the fence; but already the corner of his mouth was twitching uncontrollably. Twice he tried his long-range trick, and twice leaned backward, posed for flight, as the high horns entered his terrain. Frantically he went down on his knees for a molinete, a risky business, for it involves pirouetting on the knee caps; and foolishly he tripped, fell, and lost his muleta, which the bull carried off on its right horn. The slow handclap was heard over in the sun, and soon spread to the expensive seats; feet drummed on the boards in the boxes. Back on his feet, Litri cited for a manoletina with a new muleta, and was promptly disarmed again. The fight had dissolved into a flux of unco-ordinated mishaps. Biting his lip, he sighted along the sword and positively flung it in, as if it had been a javelin: a bad, ignoble kill. "With Litri," say the critics, "it is all or it is nothing": and this was nothing.

Vázquez made a fool of him in the third bull; he is strong in all the departments where Litri is weak. Mischievously, he led off with a polished series of naturals at long range in the Litri manner. Vázquez showed us around his shop, letting us sample an afarolado here, a molinete there, never repeating his effects but whisking them out of sight as soon as we had tasted them. He crossed over to the sunny side and, working in a space unbelievably limited, took the bull round him in *pases de la firma,* leaning on its back and chopping the muleta away from its eyes when the horns were not more than a foot past his body. Vázquez seldom sets up the emotional reverberations which Litri, at his best, achieves without trying; his music is that of the harpsicord. He had trouble with the descabello, and left the ring with only one ear, but I heard a man in the callejón say: "He is as good as his brother." Which is high praise; for although Pepe Luis Vázquez has taken his willful genius into retirement, he is still regarded by most of Spain as the connoisseur's bullfighter.

During the fight a long discussion was observed to be going on in the callejón between Luis Miguel and his father, the ex-matador Domingo González *Dominguín.* Domingo, good businessman as well as pious father, was reminding his son that the fourth bull would be his last of the feria, and that something had better be done if his reputation were to be upheld. The *diestro* was listening, rather stiffly, not looking at his father and occasionally flicking a fly from his face. His expression said: "Very well. I will extend myself. I doubt if it means anything, but I will comply." Luis Miguel is a Castilian sophisticate with social ambitions; he once made an abortive attempt to elope with the daughter of the Duke of Pinohermoso. One could see that he was offended by the necessity to prove himself before provincial Valencia. And it was thus with supreme disdain that he went out and gave the mob something to remember him by, a performance which was a ravishing digest of the whole taurine lexicon.

He was lucky in his bull, a lively lightweight which afterward tipped the scales en canal at 590 pounds. He felt his way with eight stealthy verónicas, opening the fight as Mark Twain says Tom Sawyer raised his hat, "like it was the lid of a box that had butter-flies asleep in it." Gaoneras followed, equally cautious: Luis Miguel was seeking not to be applauded but to assure himself that the bull was ripe for the firework faena he had in store for it. The picks passed without incident, and the matador put in three undemon-strative but efficacious pairs of banderillas. As he took the *trastos de matar*, the killing instruments, a wind blew up, ruffling the sand at his heels. He grimaced with annoyance.

By the end of the faena he was openly jubilant, having given a course of lectures, with lantern slides, to every aficionado in the arena. First there was a trio of right-handed passes on his knees, starting wide and easy and then bringing the bull progressively closer, like a bacon slicer whirring nearer and nearer to the thumb. Then four statuary passes, leaning precariously against the barrera; and four more derechazos, this time sitting on the *estribo*, the nar-row plank step that runs round the base of the fence. He was now ready for the left hand, with which he provoked six gracious naturals from within eighteen inches of the horns. For the first time I saw blood on Luis Miguel's stomach, and it was like seeing vomit on a queen's corsage.

His full repertoire began to unroll, even extending to six cool arrucinas. Hereabouts the bull took control of the fighter, as content is sometimes seen to dominate form, and positively in-sisted on five more naturals; Luis Miguel granted the request, and then expressed his gratitude by going down on one knee and taking the bull's horn between his teeth, a repulsive but enormously

brave adornment.* He rose, and at once plunged in a fine estocada, the best I have seen him deliver. Death was not instantaneous,
and the torero led the bull, with one hand caressing the horn, to
his natural refuge by the barrera. Slowly lumbering, submitting to
Luis Miguel's guidance, the animal found shelter, turned, and
died. The fight tapered off in a dying fall, artfully contrived and
hideously moving. Luis Miguel received both ears and the tail.

The rest of the corrida was anticlimax. In failing light Luis
Miguel scampered off with the glory of Litri's second bull by
taking it right across the ring in an interminable mariposa. Folding
the wings of his cape, he knelt and kissed the muzzle, a vulgar
attention which the bull seemed to enjoy. "See that, for Christ's
sake!" I saw Dorsey Slade twenty yards away, up on his feet, in a
fury of admiration. "He's dominated Litri's bull! He's wrecked it!
What a hypnotist!" And so it proved: the bull was now Luis
Miguel's minion and would obey no other master. The first drops
of rain were spattering down as Litri made a few tentative jabs with
the muleta, gave up and killed.

With similar wiles Luis Miguel took the edge off Vázquez's
bull, the last of the day. It withdrew from the cavalry with the
pick lodged between its shoulder blades. The professor ran in like
a flash, removed it, and put the bull through an exhausting series
of faroles, leaving it transfixed and blinking. Vázquez did his best,
but the animal was now on the defensive, a chicken-hearted giant
like Steinbeck's Lenny in *Of Mice and Men*. He dispatched it
rapidly, whereupon Luis Miguel took another bow and left the
arena in triumph. When the will to command is in him, as it was
that afternoon, there is no ace he cannot trump; he presents a
copper-plate forgery of a perfect bullfighter.

* See Plate 38, which records this moment of the faena.

I turned up my collar and hurried back toward the café in the Plaza del Caudillo. Perched on his stepladder, Vicente was moving Luis Miguel's arrow to indicate "*Colosal*"; rather like those gullible English critics who regard verse speaking, in itself a glitteringly empty skill, as the be-all and end-all of Shakespearean acting. Dorsey Slade, perambulating through the crowd with his hands plunged deep enough in his pockets to adjust his socks, here stumbled into me. He focused on me, taking his time, and said: "George, I've got to meet this joker. Lewis Miguel I mean. What a jerk! What a genius!" In the café he was dedicated and teetotal: "Just a simple lemon juice," he said squarely. Surrounded by a group of what the Spanish call North Americans, he explained that he was going to get in there with the horns "just as soon as Lewis and me have got together." Some disciplinarians of bullfight snobbism were present, and advised him not to march up to a torero and demand lessons without at least a formal introduction.

"It's bad form, see what I'm driving at?" said a florid man from Florida, with a voice like pebbles slowly rolled and a mouth no bigger than a peseta. "These guys have a *code*," he went on, as if he alone had cracked it. "They're not going to give lessons to just any bum who happens along. These guys have *class*."

Dorsey sank back in his seat, ready to spring. "Look, Aunt Emily," he said glowering, "I'll let you know when I forget about the forks and spoons."

Florida sighed, raising his eyebrows with a distinct muscular effort. "You'll learn, my boy," he said. "Why, it'd be sacrilege to bust in on Luis Miguel now. Even I wouldn't dare to do it, and I've known the guy since he was a novillero. I guess I've seen around —oh—a thousand corridas, and I want to tell you I've seen nothing like what we saw this afternoon since poor Joselito got it, and that was a *long time ago*."

Dorsey put on a bruised, shamefaced grin, which somehow presaged danger. "I guess you're right," he said, "except Lewis Miguel reminds me more of Chorro."

"I beg your pardon?" said Florida.

"Chorro," said Dorsey, "El Chorro, the Puerto Rican. Guy they used to call the Monumental Maricón."

Florida pondered, pursed his tiny mouth to the size of a pinhead and sucked sherry through it. "Never saw Chorro," he said finally, "he's just a name to me."

"El Chorro!" mused Dorsey. "The hump-backed bullfighter! The forgotten man of the ring! When Chorro died, they broke the mold. He was always getting gored, poor dope, and always with one leg up. Remember?" Dorsey jumped up, leaning backward with one leg in the air and his face twisted with pain.

"Yeah. You saw him in Mexico, was it?" said Florida, treading water.

"I was there," said Dorsey, sitting down and warming to his fantasy, "the day in Tia Juana that he invented the chorrina. The guy was bent double and crippled with gout, but my God he went out there and he invented the chorrina and it was true and honest, the way it had to be, and no laughs. Nobody else but Chorro ever made a pass sitting cross-legged with a blindfold over his face. And when you think he couldn't hardly *hobble*."

"Yeah, I saw the pictures," said Florida, "just great."

"The backward-and-sideways bit?" said Dorsey, insisting. "Two flicks and around the ears?"

"They don't come any greater," said Florida, closing the subject.

He revenged himself on Dorsey almost at once by delivering a fatuous lecture on Spanish laundries and their boundless inconvenience, all the time eying Dorsey's far-from-spotless shirt and trousers. He said he was not a snob, but that was neither here nor there: the point was to keep up appearances in a friendly foreign country, and if Dorsey would take the advice in the spirit in which it was meant, he knew of an inexpensive little peasant laundry run by an old character named Pablo who—

"I tried Pablo!" shouted Dorsey, "and look what he did to me!" Gripping his shirt front with both hands, he tugged hard, ripping off every button in a single gesture of savage self-exposure. "Perhaps this will refresh your memory?" he crooned villainously, removing his shirt altogether. Florida paled, and I felt it best to get Dorsey out of the place before he started on the furniture. He insisted on paying the bill, overtipped grossly, and left, looking slightly abject and whistling "Sierra Sue." As I followed him out of the door, he leaned heavily on my arm and said: "Now we've just *got* to meet Lewis Miguel."

I bribed a local journalist to introduce us as roving correspondents for an American picture magazine, lent Dorsey a sweater, and went with him to the Hotel Victoria. Within a few minutes of our arrival Luis Miguel sauntered down into the lounge, a slim hunter in pale-blue gabardine with a yellow scarf knotted round his neck. Dorsey stared rudely at the weak, proud mouth. I congratulated Luis Miguel on the afternoon's exploits, having first ascertained that his French was a little better than my Spanish, and then presented Dorsey to him. Thunderstruck and tongue-tied, Dorsey made a small saluting gesture and grinned.

I leaped in: "Mon ami veut savoir s'il y a des écoles où on peut étudier l'art tauromachique." Luis Miguel said there was a bullfighting school in Madrid.

I passed on the news. Dorsey brightened and asked, digging me in the ribs: "What about the little bulls? Can I get in with the little bulls?" Luis Miguel replied that tientas were rare in midsummer, and difficult to gatecrash; but he gave Dorsey full permission to mention his name to the principal at the toreros' academy in the capital. Dorsey registered awe, gratitude, and self-deprecation in one facial contortion, and then said suddenly: "Ask him how old he is." As best I could, I framed the question.

"J'ai vingt-cinq ans," said Luis Miguel, perplexed.

"What month born?" Dorsey almost bellowed.

"Le neuf décembre," said Luis Miguel politely, "et maintenant, je m'excuse, mais il y a des amis qui m'attendent, et—" He bowed and slid discreetly out. Dorsey stood leaning against a pillar, staring somberly after him.

"He was born on December 9, 1926," I said tersely.

"I know. I heard him. But I knew anyway," said Dorsey. In silence we set off for his hotel. "Do you know how I knew?" he said when we had walked about a hundred yards.

"No," I said, "but I thought it was pretty offensive of you—"

"Because," he shrieked, "I was born on the same day! Fate, Tynan! Let me tell you about fate!" He laughed uproariously in the street and skipped like a fawn. "Good night, old fellow," he said, very English, and was gone.

Next morning Dorsey Slade, spurred by the auspices and devout in his new vocation, forswore literature and entrained for Madrid to learn about the bulls. I made no attempt to dissuade him (it would have been useless) and I have not heard from him since: it is to be hoped that some fresh marshlight has taken him off course. A broken leg such as his would be a bad companion in the ring; he would have been killed at his first goring.

A year later, in New York, I telephoned his publishers, asking for news of him. "Dorsey Slade?" said the voice. "One moment,

please." There was a pause, after which I got the answer I had
secretly expected. They had never heard of him.

After the fourth corrida the competition for the Golden Ear stood
as follows: Litri had gained four trophies from four bulls (average
1), Luis Miguel had gained three from four bulls, as had Vázquez
(average o.75), and Ordóñez one from two bulls (average o.5). The
margin between the leaders was narrow, and there were two fights
to go. Yet I came to the penultimate corrida, an eight-bull affair,
with less than my usual excitement, feeling, in fact, depressed and
disconcerted. This was probably due to the curious manner in
which the previous evening had ended. After leaving Dorsey, I had
returned to the bullring to see one of the *Grandes Espectáculos
Cómicos-Taurinos-Musicales* which follow the ferias across Spain
and which, in their mixture of what our culture regards as irrec-
oncilables, have a way of turning the non-Spanish stomach.

The show begins at midnight beneath blinding arc lamps with
a march of brass bands, led round the arena by a demonstrative
conductor with a face like the Kitchener of the recruiting posters.
The audience warms to the strains of its local anthem, "Valencia."
The ring is then cleared; a trumpet sounds; and a starved little bull
—a yearling becerro—is let in, to be fought by a youthful volunteer,
aged about thirteen but arrayed in the full glory of the *traje de
luces*. There are no horses, but the rest of the ritual is micro-
scopically reproduced: capework, banderillas, and a travesty of a
faena, with the boy getting tossed again and again to shrieks of
laughter from the crowd and tearful complaints from a few pop-
eyed middle-aged women. He tries hard to kill according to the
rules, while terror counsels him to run for his life, and the result
is a sort of hit-or-miss brawl.

At length the bull dies, and the matador, burying his blushes in a nosegay, makes a hesitant circuit of the ring. Meanwhile, at lightning speed, a platform stage has been erected in mid-arena, upon which, already, a vast woman with hair like tarred rope is singing profuse flamenco into a microphone, stamping and swaying as she shouts her protestations of undying love for every rock of her native province. Unexpectedly, there are now fireworks and a selection from *Oklahoma!* by the band, whose encore consists of excerpts from the score of *Radio Follies of 1926*, played at half speed with ponderous syncopation.

The stage is then whipped away. What next? One hoped for a lady bullfighter, like the remarkable Martina García, who fought her last novillo in Madrid in 1880 at the age of seventy-six; the nineteenth century saw many *señoritas toreras*, but their vogue aroused so much controversy that in 1908 the appearance of women on foot in the bullrings of Spain was officially banned. Mexico, however, still permits it, and many a lusty Texan heiress has tried her luck in the smaller plazas close to the American border. Valencia had to make do with *charlotadas*. The band lines up by the barrera, idly playing "A Pretty Girl Is Like a Melody," and a second becerro trots into the ring. This time the clowns are the gladiators, wearing crushed toppers, baggy trousers, sequins, spurs, chaps, kilts, and pom-poms. One of them, in night shirt and night cap, feigns sleep on an iron bedstead. He snores loudly, then twitches, whereupon the little bull charges him; it is like a persecution nightmare come true. The clown jumps out of bed and, using the sheet as a cape, executes a few parody chicuelinas, and dives back again under the covers, holding his breath. The bull sniffs at him, and, wheeling suddenly, charges the musicians, who leap headlong over the barrera, leaving a sousaphone behind, which the bull gores and dents with its stubby horns.

The fight itself is a black fantasy, an absurd satanic inversion of bullfighting, as if *Everyman* were to be played by the cast of *Hellza-poppin*. Two of the comics join hands in a broadly effeminate tango, withdrawing to arm's length while the bull charges between them, and then coming amorously together again. The principal grotesque or "top banana" takes a pair of banderillas and, as he puts them in, somersaults over the horns; his partner inserts another pair and dives under the hoofs, all in one movement. One clown, in an outsize overcoat, climbs onto another's shoulders and begins the faena from a height of around nine feet. Everything, short of dressing it up in a *tutu*, is done to make the bull look foolish.

The kill, which cannot be faked or burlesqued, comes as a sickening shock; you cannot believe it is really going to happen. But the Spanish mind moves as readily as Hamlet's did from clowns to graves, and the maladroitness of the matador, who needed six thrusts to kill, was all that the crowd objected to. A mule hauls the body out and the band marches over the blood, swinging into a free arrangement of "Alice Blue Gown."

Much of comic bullfighting is brilliant and hilarious; even allowing for the smallness of the bull, there is more inventiveness in it than in nine out of ten formal corridas. But with the kill a new dimension is added; as if, in an old pantomime, Clown were to belabor Pantaloon not with a slapstick but with a crowbar. A fellow comedian is casually murdered before your eyes; the farcical tale is brutally followed through until it ends, as all tales sooner or later must end, in death.

If I am disgusted, then I stand convicted of hypocrisy. Why should one who condones bullfighting in general shrink from condoning its comic cousin? If tragedy is worth a death, why not comedy too? The history of art is full of evidence that death and cruelty are among the permanent sources of laughter; the macabre "eldritch" style of fifteenth-century Scottish poetry touches the same nerve of comedy as, in our own time, the drawings of Ronald Searle and Charles Addams. And in the drama, injuries and executions are by no means confined to tragedy; *Arsenic and Old Lace* was a riot of necrology, and until recently it was impossible to write an honest satire without a good deal of bloodshed to round it off. Jonson, Swift, and Dickens have this in common: that they can all make us laugh at savagery. The point is, of course, that they present it at one remove, the vital remove of art; comic bullfighting presents the naked thing itself. To which you might object that the cruelty in formal bullfighting is similarly naked; and I would have to agree. But the actual, visible infliction of mortal injury can never be other than a serious event. And therein lies the supreme aesthetic blunder committed by clown toreros. They get their conventions mixed. They leave the world of horseplay for the world of pain, thereby surrendering themselves to a moral law which they should never invoke.

Hence my slight unease at the next day's bullfight. It was aggravated by irrational annoyance with Julio Aparicio, who had been badly gored the week before at Palma and was thus unable to take his promised place on the cartel. I had looked forward to seeing him again: an angry, extravagant stylist, easily disgruntled, prone to hector the crowd and on occasion the president too, but a torero to the fingertips and a master of his craft. There is an ebullience of gloom as well as of joy, and this is Aparicio's. The sullen carelessness with which, after a quite, he fixes the bull at

the right, the precise, the perfect distance from the horses is one
of the minor marvels of the game. His replacement was Calerito,
so that the order of fighting now read: González, Calerito, Ordóñez,
Vázquez. The bulls were of Pablo Romero, one of the older gana-
derias (it was founded near Seville in 1888) and among the most
highly respected for the consistent beauty, caste, and courage of its
stock.

Under a sky furry with the hint of rain, I had my penultimate
view of González, who retired at the end of the season and married
shortly afterward. He was only twenty-two, but already the day was
passed in which he could be compared to Pepe Luis Vázquez except
in terms of derision. His first Pablo Romero was vast, deep-chested
and nervous; as at Pamplona, González's picador showed an astonishing willingness to be unseated. No sooner had the horns made
contact than over, like the White Knight, he spectacularly toppled.
González, trying very hard, tightened his lips and flicked out some
tentative verónicas; but it was no use. The bull dwarfed him with
its enormous contempt, its gigantic repose. Every part of the animal
breathed dignity: the proud, brooding muzzle, the bulging neck,
the dainty legs, and long, swaying brush of tail. Yet for all its
mournful calm, it could sweep into action, like an epic poem,
before you had time to blink; the bull would be moving, the armory
of horn swinging up through a semicircle, with no snort, gasp, or
effort of any kind. This was too noble an adversary for González's
twilight. He began his faena with some low right-hand passes, but
the horn cut his finger en *passant*, and that settled matters.

Giving up all pretense of combat, he killed at once to the accompaniment of a stupendous *bronca* from the crowd. The handling
of his second bull stirred up another outcry. It was little more than
a fat novillo, but one look at its wide, branching horns told me that

González could never do it justice. His faena was a gruesome cheat. He was jogged by the bull again and again, and killed it like the man in Bunyan who hacked his way into heaven after giving and receiving many wounds. One saw, and shuddered to see, a matador brutalized far below the level of the beast he sought to dominate.

Professionalism returned to the fight in the two displays of Calerito. Today he looked not (as at Pamplona) like a prizefighter but like a bronzed Hollywood cowboy of the sinister sort, walking out to the bull with as much deliberation as if he were wearing spurs, and lending the ring a momentary resemblance to the deserted street along which, in the film *High Noon*, the hero advances to meet the men who have sworn to kill him. His first bull was well cast as a murderous sharpshooter: it had a dangerous tendency to chop upward rather than lunge forward at its target. Picks and banderillas failed to correct the fault, and when Calerito began his faena with three statuary passes, the horns were surging up through the cloth to a height of about seven feet. Judging the neck muscles sufficiently tired, he shook the cloth for a natural, at which I shivered; surely he would emerge with a gashed face and concussion? But he didn't; sheer nerve, that extra inch of sombre panache which seems to grow in Córdoba pulled him through, and from a bull one had thought unteachable he extracted not one but a dozen naturals, each lower and closer than the last. Hesitance gave place to fluency; oil was being applied to a stiff and rusty machine. He capped his naturals with manoletinas and high derechazos, killed with an eclipsing estocada right out in mid-ring, and carried off both ears and the tail.

Calerito likes to fight with the odds against him. His second faena, in the sixth bull, was an example of what theater critics call "struggling in vain with inadequate material." This time the trouble was a pronounced hook with the left horn, in spite of which Calerito insisted on citing for left-hand naturals. The results were not pretty, but they were certainly thrilling; only acute mental geometry and exquisite timing kept the man on his feet. The bull was not charging in a straight line but on a bias toward the left, so that every pass was a violent emotional ordeal for both fighter and audience, too naked in its violence to be classed as first-rate bullfighting. The war of nerves ended with a fine kill, and Calerito again received the ears and tail.

This of course decided the outcome of the competition for the Golden Ear, since Calerito, who was engaged for only one corrida, had achieved an average of three amputations per bull, which nobody else could hope to challenge. A total outsider, landing as it were by parachute, had callously sprinted past the post. Nevertheless, it would be no reflection on Calerito's prestige to say that it didn't much matter, to the Valencians or to myself. The larger issue, between Litri and Ordóñez, remained open. For us, at that point in bullfighting history, nothing else counted.

Ordóñez gave the Litristas some bad shocks with his first Pablo Romero. After we had toiled up Calerito's cobbled hill, this was like walking on green resilient turf again; a holiday after the hard work of term. Six verónicas, dexterously pert, were the hors d'œuvres, finished off with a vivid *rebolera*, that gay extension of the half verónica which whisks the cape behind the man's back like a dancer's skirt. Each pass shone like a line from a medieval lyric, with the rebolera appended as a genial *envoi*. Ordóñez emphasizes the continuity of bullfighting; he is refining an existing tradition, where Litri is an isolated and unheralded freak. After this filigree work with the cape, Ordóñez's faena seemed plain and unadorned, and I began to realize the truth of a Madrid critic's comment that "his cape was made in Seville and his muleta in Ronda." He built on a solid bedrock of naturals, sustained and encouraged by an excellent bull, and the strength of the faena was such that its flourishes, when they came in the shape of molinetes and arrucinas, served properly to enhance the solemnity of the design. From each group of passes he walked away breathless, his round, puckered face expressing the delight of an adolescent in the grip of calf love. Except that bull love would be a better term. Fighting bulls intoxicates Ordóñez; the pleasure of carrying out the pattern of a fine faena glows in his eyes. He "feels at each thread, and lives along the line." Aesthetics in bullfighting is a matter of inches, of the smallest nuances; the curve in which the horns are taken past the body depends on the nicest calculation. Many fighters are capable of the calculation, but few, apart from Ordóñez, can communicate the creative joy which accompanies it.

Having duly preened himself, he raised the sword and killed—honorably, for him, and cleanly, though I doubt whether Luis Freg or Mazzantini would have approved. Killing is the only branch of his craft in which Ordóñez has, so to speak, torn up yesterday, abandoned tradition and schooled himself in the safe, bad habits of modern practice.

The treatment of his second bull drove home a sore but vital point: that bullfighting, like the cinema, is a collective craft, all the elements of which must be in harmony before it can become a means of personal expression. The preparation of the bull by peons and picadors can destroy it just as surely as a cowardly producer and an incompetent cameraman can destroy a good story. But while a director can, if he is lucky, withdraw from a setup he dislikes, a matador is committed to his bull. And the difference in quality between bulls is much wider than the difference between fighters;

a second-rate matador can put up a better showing with a good bull than a first-rate matador with a bad one.

Ordóñez's second bull was a good one, the most attractive of the corrida (it dressed out at 700 pounds), until, in a show of excessive caution, his script writers got to work on it. You might say that they broke the back of the story with the cape and then took the heart out of it with the picks. The tamed, censored creature which came to the muleta was changed beyond recognition. What followed proved once more that a bullfight depends on the condition of the bull as no football game ever depended on the condition of the ball. Ordóñez did his best to improve matters with a long faena which called up every pass in the book, but which amounted, critically speaking, to little more than a gorgeous baroque pediment with no pillars to support it. A curious footnote might be added. I pointed out to my neighbor a large white V on the bull's muzzle; he nodded and said that Manolete had killed a similarly marked animal at Valencia in 1942 and sent its stuffed head to Winston Churchill. The Prime Minister's letter of thanks, congratulating the matador on his emergence from "what was clearly a hazardous encounter," now hangs framed in Camará's office.

My last sight, that year, of Manolo Vázquez. The erratic manikin was not at his best: his first bull was not brave enough for him, his second far too brave. Ordóñez's style is eclectic and hence adaptable, but Vázquez is a Sevillian specialist who needs bulls that fit him like a second skin. Give him a misfit, and he looks silly, if not actually contemptible. He and his first bull, a coward, made a rapid and disgraceful compact: neither would come within a yard of the other, and the execution would be quick. That it wasn't can scarcely be held against Vázquez. As he was in the act of killing, close to the barrera, the gaudy yellow-shirted shoulders of an American photographer loomed up over the fence. The sudden movement and the whir of the camera distracted the bull, which swung to the right, and Vázquez narrowly escaped being impaled through his navel. The intruder grinned and waved a massive paw in quite inadequate self-deprecation. Understandably Vázquez was shaken, and the estocada, when at last he delivered it, was wide of the mark.

The last bull looked like the last bull on earth, an ugly, inbred monster and a throwback to the squat, antenna-horned creatures in Goya's aquatints. It was a dappled gray, the color of the rain-laden sky above it, with a jet-black nose. Yet its *nobleza* was apparent as soon as it bustled into sight, to none more clearly than to the *espontáneo* who immediately vaulted in from the cheap side of the ring. This emaciated child, perhaps fourteen years old, pulled from under his shirt, where it had probably been hidden throughout every fight of the feria, a stick and a rag tacked together to make a muleta. He cited for a right-handed pass, puffing out his chest. To our consternation, the bull charged; to our delight, the trick worked. The boy, unquestionably a Litrista, stared up at his friends in the boxes as he brought off an admirable derechazo with an unpicked bull.

His pride was haunting. The big gray turned and charged again, and he repeated the pass, in excellent style, with his feet together and not more than six inches of daylight between his belly and the horns. The olés were sounding as he lined up for the third pass; and then came calamity. The right horn removed the muleta from his grasp and he was left weaponless, with the peons running in to bundle him from the ring. He stamped his foot in fury; you would have thought him a poet whose nib had crossed in the middle of a line. There were tears in his saucer eyes, and his long, prehensile nose twitched in agony. What to do? The answer visibly burst upon him, and in a moment of superb theatricality he tore off his shirt and called on the bull to attack him again. By then it was too late; its attention had been drawn elsewhere. He was still gripping his shirt as if for a verónica when the peons caught him under the shoulders and dragged him half naked to the fence, his sandaled feet leaving parallel trails in the sand. We cheered uproariously, and hissed when they handed him over to the civil guard.

When an espontáneo proves that he possesses both courage and skill, most matadors grow resentful. Picasso, I imagine, must feel the same if he ever reads those letters to the newspapers in which parents boast that their six-year-old children are just as clever as he at the technique of non-objective art. Vázquez relapsed into torpor at once; his face froze into a mask of scorn. The bull, refreshed by its skirmish, launched a tremendous assault on the horses; but the faena lasted less than two minutes. As Vázquez plodded out of the arena, a Napoleon in bitter retreat, the audience whistled and jeered. A few drops of rain fell on their vast dissatisfaction.

Later that evening an impromptu cabaret was held outside one of the cafés in the Plaza del Caudillo. Manolo Berris, a comely, wakeful four-year-old, had added a new item to his repertoire of impersonations. I had already seen and admired his mimicry of boxers, airplanes, policemen, and homosexuals; now this gifted child turned to bullfighting, and gave us his version of the chagrin and defeat of Manolo Vázquez. We applauded; and, having pummeled his elder sister with glee, he ran round the square whooping and crept back to accept the offer of an ice-cream soda. Why, we asked, was he so interested in bullfighting? Because, he said, drooling chocolate, he had been taught that Spain was shaped like the spread-out skin of a bull, and if God had made Spain like that, He must have meant that good Spaniards and good bulls belonged together.

I went back to the hotel. The streets were by now blue with dawn. Litri and Ordóñez were asleep, but the day of their combat had begun.

8

The Challenge:
Litri and Ordóñez

Is THE fall of a leaf beautiful in itself? Or is it beautiful only when a poet has written about it or an artist painted it? We still argue the question; that we do so is part of the heritage of humanism, which laid it down as an axiom that a polished and elevated style could transmute base metal into gold, a dead leaf into a poetic image. In culinary terms, humanism impressed on our culture the notion that beauty was the difference between raw meat and *entrecôte bordelaise*. The consequence is that nowadays we find it hard to accept the idea that an accident of nature can be beautiful. We think it a sentimental fallacy. Beauty, as we define it, happens not by chance but by an act of will on the part of an artist, working with a controlled purpose and knowing exactly what he is about. The falling leaf is beautiful, if at all, for a few seconds in a certain light; if it is to last, to be more durable than iron, to be a bastion against transience, it must be recorded in print, paint, or celluloid.

Interpretative artists, such as actors and bullfighters, stand in especial need of observers to immortalize them. For a decade or two they may achieve a frail survival on men's lips, but thereafter they are in the hands of the artists who were their contemporaries, as

Hazlitt was Edmund Kean's. Now mark a strange thing about the history of dramatic criticism. It is the great imperfect actors who chiefly live in its pages, the intense romantics, the Keans, Irvings, and Salvinis; and not the perfect, explicit, classical performers like John Philip Kemble and Betterton. Those who reached, rather than those who grasped, have been our critics' darlings and made their pens run purple. The critic-artist is naturally drawn to those players who achieve what seems to be accidental and unpremeditated beauty, needing the refinement of art to attain its fullest expression. Criticism seeks to complete the process, to push it, as C. E. Montague said, "one stage further in definiteness and intensity" so that the result is "an arch of feeling crowned at last"—art, in a word. He may admire the actors whose effects are perfectly judged and timed, but their very perfection chills him; they do not need his help; they are already brought to birth. Give him the actor who make a thunderous effect without appearing to know how or why he is making it; whose magnetism is such that he can disembowel his audience without being aware that he has made so much as an incision: give him, in short, the actor who doesn't know his own strength. I do not say that performances like Olivier's Oedipus, Marlon Brando's Stanley Kowalski, or Wilfred Lawson's "The Father" were wonders only of instinct and accident: the point is that they *seemed* so. The actors seemed to be working in the dark and tripping over beauty, as a man may stumble by night on a gold mine which patient daylight toilers have sought for months in vain.

All of which leads me straight into the great final bullfight of the Valencian fair, when Reach was confronted with Grasp, Accident with Design, Romantic with Classic, *Sturm und Drang* with Age of Gold; Litri, in fact, with Ordóñez. They met on equal terms: each had so far killed four bulls during the feria, and gained four trophies. The antithesis between their methods was exactly that which I have outlined between the nocturnal stumbler and the sunlit toiler. With Litri beauty is a by-product of neurosis. He must prove something to the onlookers; must show that a poor starveling can dominate and kill. That a faena may be a beautiful thing has never occurred to him; he is too close to his work, too emotionally over-wrought by it. Ordóñez, on the other hand, stands apart. He is intent only on shaping a sequence of passes, according to the rules, which shall be graceful, firm, and thrilling. He improves the more he learns, whereas Litri declines. When Litri discovered that it was possible to reduce his methods to technical terms, his faith in himself waned abruptly; that of Ordóñez, in similar circumstances, swelled and prospered. Litri is the child who can hit a tin can with a stone at twenty yards until someone teaches him the laws of trajectory and propulsion, after which the gift atrophies. Which would prevail, the flawed visionary or the peerless pragmatist? We gathered at the bullring to find out.

Juan Pedro Domecq, the breeder, had sent along six exceptional bulls, none of them a giant, but all fast, bold, and persistent in attack. This meant a fight which would, given good toreros, conform to the right pattern, to preserve which from abolition the Spanish have battled against Church and Government for two centuries. Within a few hours of the last bull's death, the singers of the coast were proclaiming the afternoon's adventures; next day the newspapers were hymning them, and Manolo Berris, oblivious of hostile traffic signals, was hopping round the square, squealing in a private ecstasy, rolling his eyes, uttering bird cries, and expressing, as far as his childhood could, the liberating joy of a fine corrida.

The sky was churned to the color of porridge when the bullring clock touched five-thirty. The paseo began, and the rain with it, thinly at first, but soon amplified into a downpour. This was Gray's "iron-sleet of arrowy shower"; and "arrowy" exactly conveys the whistling, whipping wind which shuddered the flags around the edge of the plaza. The matadors marched in triple file across to the president's box: Manolo González on the right, Litri on the left, and Ordóñez between them. A vocal grimace of complaint at once arose from the crowd, who wanted the fight postponed until a finer day. Normally the president would have agreed, and promised that within ten days a corrida of equal prestige would be organized; meanwhile entrance money would have been returned. But during a feria things are different; the town will not be so full of afición in ten days' time, and there are considerable financial risks in postponement. So the trumpet blew, and the first Domecq bull, its pink and white ribbons dancing in its shoulders, bounded out of the toril gate.

It was handled like the dull but necessary exposition of a play, before the entrance of the stars. González and his picador, José Márquez, did all they could to intimidate the enemy, which took five heavy picks, but when they had finished there was still enough skittish courage left in the bull to have made a wonderful fight. An ancient reflex stirred in González, and he gave his best performance of the fair, neat but not gaudy and confident without arrogance. He offered his stomach to the bull and drew the horns past him four times with the muleta, which he swept back in the right way, like a man pulling open a low drawer. The naturals were followed by an exciting group of manoletinas and passes en redondo, all of a valor and slickness which amazed me. The wetness of the sand soon began to disturb him, though; he was obviously fearful of slipping. Rain was trickling off his nose as he went in to kill, and when, pricked by the descabello, the bull dropped in its tracks, a great roll of thunder racketed round the silent arena.

As the second bull came in for Litri, leftover thunder was still rumbling and rain audibly spattered the sand. We were balancing cushions on our heads, and it was touch and go whether we would stay. The little man shot a sour glance round the ring before running out to make the decision for us: eight sparkling, swooping verónicas, scarcely moving his feet, after which it would have been folly to leave. The bull went for the horse like a wolf on the fold, and the picador, Pimpi, rose to the occasion with a single pick, long but perfectly placed.* Nobody could doubt now that the situation held some danger; the bull was losing its footing, and the sky was darkening rapidly; a feel of gods'-twilight, sticky and angry, hung over the arena.

And Litri was defying both bull and tempest, first in a series of derechazos close to the barrera, looking daggers of accusation at the crowd, and then in a chest pass and six fierce manoletinas, out in the middle. Anxiety was hardening into determination; the insect was really roused. Some of the passes left feet of air between him and the horns, but it was fantastic, in this cloudburst, to be passing the bull at all. The band struck up in his honor, a whip-cracking pasodoble. Litri stamped his thin foot, citing for a seventh manoletina, passed the bull beneath his right arm and, as he turned, took the horn straight in his left buttock. The bull had slipped and veered too quickly. Litri fell between the forelegs and slumped, covering his face with his arms until a peon's cape took the bull away; and then, scratched and livid with pride, bounded to his feet, stretched upon tiptoe, and ripped in with the sword. He leaned nervelessly across the horns, knowing as we knew that the estocada

* This is the pick represented in Plate 19.

was perfect, and sprang back to watch the bull tilt and topple. As it did so, every fuse in the world blew: a river of forked lightning flowed across the sky. It was a moment of operatic hallucination. Litri was given the bull's ears for the kind of courage which is his specialty: courage in circumstances where classical bullfighting is an impossibility and grace an implausible accident. His faena was tauromachy stripped to the skin.

Ordóñez, wiping the rain out of his eyes, went out to meet the third bull, a burly black with a streak of lion-brown along its spine, in a spirit of gay emulation. Kicking off his slippers to get a firmer foothold in the ooze, he embarked on a fight which started as a parody of Litri's and then developed into a demonstration of how the thing should really be done. The big Domecq took five picks without any effort, but after one pair of banderillas Ordóñez changed the thirds and began his faena with six passes in precise and mordant imitation of the Litri manner.

Holding the muleta in his right hand, pricked out as wide as possible by the sword, he swung the bull past him at arm's length, taking no risks at all and ramming the joke home by shading his eyes with his left hand as if the bull were a dot on the horizon. He accompanied each pass with the characteristic Litri scowl of tragic dominion. But even as we laughed he changed tactics, switched the muleta to his left hand and gave us six of his own inimitable naturals, the real thing, low and lingering and filled with a jubilant seriousness. The five molinetes which came next were aureate, "enamellit" bullfighting at its most joyous. The molinete is a pass based on secure knowledge of tangents. With the muleta in the right hand, you cite the bull and, when it charges, pirouette anticlockwise on one foot, wrapping the cloth round your body like a corpse wrapped in a flag on the battlefield. The horn cuts past you

as you spin, brushing against the muleta-swathed hip, straight line
against circle, tangent against perimeter. Ordóñez did this five
times to a miracle. For an encore he mocked Litri again, this time
with manoletinas; when the charge came, he stared up at the clouds
with a puzzled expression which said, as clearly as a balloon in a
comic strip: "Looks like rain." He then ruined everything by killing badly (three attempts); but the ovation was so prolonged and
the waving of handkerchiefs so persistent that the president had to
award an ear.

Water now stood in pools across the ring, and the rain had settled
down to a miserly drizzle. The tension slackened: we remembered
to shiver, and cognac flasks passed from mouth to mouth. Meanwhile González was going through the motions of fighting the
fourth bull, a portly beige creature, and making a rotten job of it.
The bull was slow, Manolo had no heart for it, and the interlude
was soon over. This was his farewell performance in Valencia, but
you would not have guessed it from the slack and casual way in
which he killed: the necks of chickens have been wrung with more
dignity. When the body had been dragged out and González had
made his unwept exit from the Valencian plaza, a thunderbolt black
shot into sight, charged at a flicker of cape, and splintered the tip
of its left horn against the burladero. It stood questing, begging for
trouble, daring any man to sneeze in its presence: a perfect Domecq
bull, which is as close as zoology can get to a tank.

Out in a wondering reverie came Litri, committed—it soon appeared—to chicuelinas, but chicuelinas of a pattern so curious that
Chicuelo might not have owned them. He shook the cape as for a
normal verónica; the bull wheeled and plunged toward him; and
when its whole body had passed by, he spun round on his toes, in a
superfluous revolution. He looked abstracted and tentative; but I

could tell from the shrill commands that flowed from him when the bull took its first pick—royally, monumentally—that his heart had leaped up. The horses were instantly removed, and the peons placed only one pair of sticks; brushing them from his path Litri stalked out, sure of himself, and dedicated the bull to Valencia, to Andalusia, and to the world. The tempo of the corrida had quickened; it was bouncing now, striding along, taking all hurdles of prejudice at a gallop. As Litri walked toward the bull with the sword in one hand and the furled muleta in the other, I prayed for the president of the S.P.C.A. to materialize at my elbow, so that I might convert him.

Facing that fifth bull, Litri embodied all that the human race dislikes about itself—its spite, its wrath, its ineradicable guilt. Ordóñez, by contrast, embodies all that we pride ourselves on—our grace, our intellect, our generosity. Litri's courage is derived from despair; Ordóñez's, from hope. Ordóñez is one of the elect, Litri one of the damned, yet out of his purgatory he summoned up a terrible valor which took him to the perihelion of his neurotic powers. He seemed to be willing his own death. Six bleak, still statuaries opened the faena, after which he plodded away to the opposite fence, sang out his challenge, and took the full impetus of the charge on his yielding muleta, furled in the left hand; the bull was trapped, held, mesmerized, and followed the folded cloth through eight naturals, crowned with a releasing chest pass. Then— outrageously—three more naturals, with the torero's eyes tightly shut.

The rain fell with doubled force; the sun sulked elsewhere, but Litri was its deputy. Out in the middle of the swamp he completed seven burning derechazos, and then as many reckless manoletinas. He would not be content with a graze or a mere goring: this was life or death. Now he was on his knees, still waving the muleta and refusing to move, and eight times the bull passed him and granted him life. He was past caring now, past hearing even, though the olés must have been heard at the beach, miles away down the dripping streets. When the bull had skimmed under his arm for the eighth time, he threw his sword to the left and his muleta to the right and, turning, stroked the brave black muzzle. Still kneeling, he then stretched his hands out to us in a gesture of supplication.* There was a look of inexorable pity in his eyes as he rose, gathered up his tools, and killed in a swift, clear thrust.

In a second the ring was white with handkerchiefs. The ears and the tail were not enough; the cheers did not subside until a hoof had been cut as well, and Litri had made two triumphant circuits of the ring. "Give him the head!" yelled an incensed anti-Litrista. "Give him the cojones too!" Shuffling in the treacherous sand, Litri nodded his acceptance of the ovation.† This had been his patent faena, with the stamp of his personality on every second of it. There are dramatic critics who complain that the actor has eclipsed the drama; similarly, there are bullfight critics who complain that the torero has eclipsed the bullfight. It seems a valid objection, until you see someone like Litri, in whom the corrida is so violently epitomized that you wonder that there was ever bullfighting before him.

Ordóñez made the only reply in his power. He answered intensity with copiousness. There was no chance now of his equaling Litri's record of ten trophies in six bulls unless, as was frankly unthinkable, he cut two hoofs of the last bull. With invincible élan he threw himself into what proved to be the best long fight I have

* This moment of the faena is caught in Plate 43.
† Plate 57.

ever seen. Litri had shown us the XYZ of bullfighting raised to its highest emotional power; Ordóñez gave us the ABC as well. He stationed himself on his knees about twelve paces away from the toril gate, the damp magenta of his cape gleaming before him and then whirling around his head as the bull came charging in, passing within a foot of his left shoulder. Swiveling on his knees, he repeated the maneuver: another magnificent *larga cambiada*. Rising, he ran out into mid-ring and, rooted in the squelching sand, took the bull through eight fluent, meditative verónicas. We had held our breath for Litri; now we could breathe deeply and easily, so secure did the young maestro seem. While the ovation sounded, he lined the bull up for the horses, one of which was thrown at first impact. There, in a flash, was Ordóñez, beckoning the horns to join him in four lucid gaoneras. One pick and one pair of banderillas were enough: the bull was in the same state of preparation as Litri's had been.

The next ten minutes were a digest of all the fables in which a princely hero subdues a legendary monster. With the difference that Theseus, as far as we know, had good weather in which to defeat the minotaur; Ordóñez's exploit had more in common with Beowulf's submarine triumph over Grendel. Almost you could say that he waded, certainly that he splashed his way out with the sword and the cloth. To shoot the bull dead with a pistol would have been hard enough in that light; to fight it as he did, progressively and with the utmost pictorial beauty, was definably insane. Never stepping back, and shifting his ground only by choice, he drove the enemy back into its castle, the center of the ring, and there put it to the sword. It was Jack the Giant Killer all over again, with his valor purified by art.

Even slipperless, he could scarcely keep his balance; yet he began the faena by removing his montera, placing it at his feet and putting his toes inside it.* Thus he announced to us that the fight would take place on ground of his choosing, from which he would not be dislodged. Muleta and sword hung like a sloped flag from his outstretched arms. The bull charged once, and turned; charged again, and turned; charged again to complete three flawless statuary passes, which, when El Gallo performed them, were known as passes of the Celestial Empire. This was metrical bullfighting; the rhythm of the passes kept pace with a primordial pulse. Advancing from the barrera, he cited from twenty yards for a right-handed, aided pass, and, having suavely accomplished it, coiled the bull round him in five more of the like.

His calm was ecstatic; visions of Watteau portraits crossed the mind, expelling the Bosch-like nightmares of Litri. Farther still from the fence, he moved over to the left hand, and in a serene feat of traction pulled the horns through six respectful naturals, as if they had been on the end of an elastic cord. The bulk of the bull passed him each time from horn to tail; nothing was skimped or fumbled. Five more naturals, and a chest pass; a trio of life-juggling molinetes; and he was in the heart of enemy country, erect in the middle of the ring.

The fight telescoped out, growing longer and grander, but with its proportions ever harmonious. Each pass was practical as well as pretty. The foundation of classical naturals was firm; the superstructure of the rest was gratuitous beauty. To change the metaphor, you could read him for the moral as well as for the style. As he went in to kill, lightning flared again, and the sword went in and out in a metisaca. This was bad luck, which he instantly rectified with solid technique. His second thrust, veiled by a crossing left hand, buried the steel up to the hilt. He followed the sword home with his body

* Pictured in Plate 28.

so far that the horn caught him in the crotch and bumped him to the ground; but the bull was dead before he climbed to his feet.

The mortal, with sublime hubris, had conferred mortality on the beast, which we had seen aging before us, growing out of its lusty childhood and maturing, in the face of honorable challenge, until it was tired and ripe for death. Rapture swept the entire plaza. The instructed artist, working within the tradition, had us at his feet. With the ears in one hand and the tail in the other, Ordóñez was swept shoulder high round the ring,* and the mayoral of the Domecq ranch rose in his seat to respond to the cheers. For Valencia, perhaps, it was Litri's day; but for the afición at large, it was Ordóñez's year.

I have said that good bullfighting sends my mind to the epic. That evening I opened Pope's translation of the *Iliad* for the first time since leaving Oxford, and found in his preface an analysis of the ways in which "poetical fire" reveals itself in its votaries. At once a procession of matadors filed into my thoughts. "This Fire," says Pope, "is discern'd in Virgil, but discern'd through a Glass, reflected, and more shining than warm, but everywhere equal and constant": here was Luis Miguel. "In Lucan and Statius," Pope goes on, "it bursts out in sudden, short and interrupted Flashes": here were Vázquez, perhaps, and Calerito. "In Milton, it glows like a Furnace kept up to a uncommon Fierceness by the Force of Art": Ordóñez, for sure. "In Shakespeare it strikes before we are aware, like an accidental Fire from Heaven": who else but Litri? "But in Homer," Pope concludes, "and in him only, it burns everywhere clearly, and everywhere irresistibly." There was never a bullfighter like this, or if there was, I have not seen him, or read about him. This is not to say

* See Plate 58.

that he will never exist. He may be growing up as I write this, may even be laying plans for his debut; in which case I shall hear of him, the word will be passed through the international web of aficionados, and the pilgrimages will begin again, to Seville in the spring, to Madrid in May, to Pamplona and Valencia in high summer. What will his name be? As I write, it might be Chamaco, or Cascales, or Bernadó. Or perhaps they will turn out to be chimeras like the rest. We shall keep watching.

"But Homer, indeed!" I can hear many good Englishmen snorting. "Milton! And Shakespeare!" And I agree that I have not written coolly about the bullfight, nor would I if I could. I have preferred to be immoderate and go to extremes: I would mistrust any man who could talk about Spain in a monotone. Of course matadors, even the greatest, rank lower in the hierarchy than poets; but my analogy is not thereby destroyed. Though different in degree, they are of the same party. They are makers. Out of shapelessness they conjure a shape, one which I like to contemplate as much as I like to see Chekhov, to read Thomas Browne or Hopkins, to hear Bix Beiderbecke, or to imagine Edmund Kean.

The bullfight has never shocked me as it shocked the retired brigadier who, when I wrote a piece about it in a newspaper, sent a postcard to the editor recommending that people who used their passports for such arcane purposes should have them removed and be clapped for a month into jail. Like many other members of the first adult generation since the war, I look on violence as part of my condition, and would rather have it in a bullring, ordered and codified, than on a battlefield. With those who cannot sympathize, I do not argue. Where the bulls are concerned there is no point in preaching except to the converted.

And what happened to Litri and Ordóñez? Neither of their stories is yet over. In 1953 Ernest Hemingway saw Ordóñez for the first time, and said he was as good as the very best. At the end of the season he married Luis Miguel's pretty, dark-haired younger sister and firmly announced his retirement; but in 1954 he was still fighting, and frequently touching the heights of 1952*—emulating the master, Luis Miguel, he has even taken to putting in his own banderillas. A pack of ambitious novilleros are now at his heels, among them his younger brother José, who had a triumphant presentation in Madrid during the San Isidro Fair of 1954. About Antonio's future I would not care to prophesy. As John Marks has written: "The modern matador's day fades as swiftly as a Spanish evening."

The case of Litri is more provocative. In October, 1952, three months after the Valencian Fair and a few days after his twenty-second birthday, he retired from the bulls, taking his farewell in a *mano a mano* with Pedrés, on whom he bestowed the alternativa. He made a few charity appearances in 1953, one of them at Madrid, where the warmth of the applause brought tears to his eyes; but he has not fought for money since. His first act in retirement was to buy a house, an old Andalusian mansion on the main residential street of Huelva. A firm of Madrid decorators was engaged to strip and refurbish it, which was done at a cost of $30,000; the place was transformed into a profusion of chandeliers, antique furniture and silver plate, with mounted bulls' heads and portraits of the young seigneur gazing down on marble floors. Here he ignored the press, which clamored and clamors still to know why he gave up his *métier*. Why, having so recently proved that his powers had not

* Ordóñez more than agrees with this estimate. At the end of the 1954 season he was invited by an interviewer to name the six best bullfighters on the active list. He replied: "Sixth, Jumillano. Fifth, Girón. Fourth, either Antoñete or Pedrés. Third, Antonio Bienvenida. Second, Julio Aparicio. First, Antonio Ordóñez."

diminished, did he abandon the ring after four short years? His mother, who manages the household and copes with her son's correspondence, piously believes that it was for her sake. An impassioned matriarch whose deep, crestfallen eyes Miguel has inherited, she has no doubts about his motives: "I have been father, mother, everything to him, and like a good child he has rewarded me. He leaves the bulls alone because he wants me to be at peace." Litri's sister, a lively hoyden, shares her mother's opinion.

There are other, less romantic views of the matter. Some say that Camará, who dominated Litri's professional life so completely that often he had no idea how much he was earning, advised him to retire at a peak rather than slide into decline. Others, pointing out that Litri was always shy of fighting Miuras, insist that he took fright when horn shaving was outlawed, but the truth is that he announced his retirement long before Bienvenida's campaign began. I have also heard it said that he had a vocation for the priesthood, a theory scoffed at by his mother and sister. Yet he was undoubtedly among the most superstitious members of a superstitious profession. When fighting, he used to pack three images of the Virgin in his baggage, and the Virgin of the Sash, who guards Huelva, has a shrine in his bedroom, her vestment adorned with gold thread unpicked from one of his costumes. Even so, I agree with his family that he could never be a true contemplative. His mission, which is now accomplished, was to prove that one of his family could leave the ring famous and whole, not scarred like his father, not dead like Manuel.

Unless he returns to the game (and he probably will: matadors are like prima donnas), a desert of ennui stretches ahead of him. He entertains seldom and hates it, smiling wanly and looking extremely uncomfortable. He sips whisky from time to time, without much enthusiasm, and is a moderate dancer. On occasion he has played inside right for the local amateur football club. He once tried to persuade me that he read only history and biography, but the idea convulsed his sister: nothing, she said, but outdoor magazines and adventure stories. Like Manolete, he is a good shot. He rides well and has two horses; drives well and has two cars; sails well and has two boats. Above all, he has the torero's passion for cock fighting. He owns twenty bantams, mostly English bred, and the only time I have ever seen him carefree was at a cock fight in Madrid, betting on his own birds. Frail, toothpick-thighed and markedly knock-kneed, he is always stirred by the smell of combat.

The ambassadorial opulence of his home does not impress him much. He bought it primarily for his mother and sister, and is usually out, sitting in silence at a corner bar, sipping a manzanilla and shrugging the corners of his mouth as his friends make jokes for him. Once he was summoned to Madrid to dine with the Caudillo. Loyalty demanded his presence, and he went; but by the first train he was back in Huelva, twiddling his thumbs and nursing his secret. His usual companion is Galápago, who was one of his peons. A peasant with the face of a flushed chimpanzee, Galápago had eyesight so poor that sooner or later a bull must have caught him. Aware of this, and aware, too, that he could not afford to retire, Litri brought him back to Huelva, where he was born, and gave him a pension for life. I found this out by chance, from a man in a café; no one I know has more pride in the ring and less out of it than Litri.

His mother's most ardent wish is that he should marry decently, "a good woman, not one of these clever modern wives," and then settle down to farming. If it is denied and he comes back to the ring, I have a feeling that it will be without much heart for the job.

It was in his fourth season that Manuel was killed; Miguel, having seen four seasons through, may have decided that the family's luck has been tried far enough. I hope, for his sake, that he remains a recluse. His life has been governed by honor, pacts, and promises— to himself, to his mother, and to the Virgin. When he became a matador he promised the Virgin of Rocío, whose shrine is seventy kilometers from Huelva, that if he was preserved he would make a pilgrimage to her. In May, 1954, he made good the pledge, riding across open country for two days to the shrine, where he gave thanks for his life and luck. He also undertook to repeat the journey every year until he died. His contract with the bulls, for the moment, is over. His contract with the Virgin is for life.

Epilogue

THERE has been much about death in this book, but it has been the death of bulls, not of men. All the matadors in it are still, as I write, alive and glad to be; some of them, a little startled to be. To balance the picture, it may be well to remind the reader of a disaster, which he is at liberty to call a retribution, if he is so minded. What follows, then, is a plain account, factually derived from Francisco Narbona's *Manolete* and Don Luis's *Toros y Toreros 1947 a 1950*, of the sequence of events which culminated in Linares, a small industrial town just south of the Sierra Morena in Andalusia, on August 28, 1947.

Manuel Rodriguez "Manolete" had entered his thirty-first year on July 4. His birthplace was Córdoba, 190 miles down the Guadalquivir from Linares. Since 1939 he had been at the height of his profession; lean, hawk-nosed and saturnine, he was dubbed "The Monster," and the national idolatry he commanded was greater even than that accorded to Belmonte. The gossips said that the incessant strain of having to be always at his best had lately been driving him to the bottle; Camará, his agent and friend, had confessed that he often seemed a somnambulist, so badly was he weakened by late hours and deep drinking.

On July 16, fighting unpaid in a charity corrida at Madrid, he had been gored by a Bohórquez bull and, although swaying on his feet,

completed the faena and kill before consenting to be carried to the
infirmary, where the bull's ears were brought to him. His con-
valescence took three weeks and meant the cancellation of six contracts. On August 4, still groggy, he reappeared at Vitoria, cutting an
ear. He fought again in the same town on the 5th, and traveled
during the next ten days to Valdepeñas, San Sebastian, Huesca, and
Gijon; in all four places he seemed ominously shaky. On the 16th
he returned to San Sebastion on the same program as Luis Miguel,
his most serious rival among the younger men, and cut both ears of
his first bull. As the cheers died, he was asked by a radio commenta-
tor in the callejón to say a few words. He responded laconically:
"They ask of me more than I can give. I would say only one thing,
and that is that I wish it were October and the season were ended."
He failed in the second bull, and the crowd jeered. That evening he
dined with his mother, and then departed for Toledo, where he had
a spectacular success on the 17th.

A few days later he gave an interview to a journalist in which
he said he had decided to retire at the end of the year. "I am out of
temper," he said. "The public expects more of me every time I
appear. It is impossible." Before a hostile audience in Gijon on the
24th he was lamentably bad, and two days later, at Santander, he
heard only mild applause. Meanwhile, the posters were already up
in Jaen and Córdoba and the villages of the Guadalquivir valley,
announcing the cartels for the feria at Linares. Two corridas had
been organized, in the first of which, fixed for the 28th, Gitanillo de
Triana, Manolete, and Luis Miguel would meet six Miura bulls.

On the evening of Wednesday the 27th, Manolete left Madrid
by car, accompanied by Camará, a bullfight journalist named Bellón,
and Guillermo, his chauffeur-cum-swordhandler. They arrived in

Linares soon after dawn next day, having driven all night, and
Manolete went straight to his room to rest. At eleven he rose; the
hubbub of a town en fête welled up from the streets. He breakfasted
lightly on fruit, and received handshakes from a few friends. The
fight was timed to begin at five-thirty; around four he put on the
suit of lights and, after a few minutes of prayer, rose and faced
Camará.

"How are the bulls, Pepe?"

"Fine. Not too big, not too little."

At five-fifteen he was driven to the bullring, looking as bleak and
impassive as always.

The Plaza de Toros at Linares, officially classified as a second-
category ring, holds ten thousand spectators. It was full to over-
flowing. The three matadors were greeted with an ovation, to acknowledge which Manolete led them out, montera in hand, to the
middle of the circle. Gitanillo, a once-brilliant gypsy, two years
Manolete's senior and for many years his friend, took the first Miura.
It lacked power, but was frank with the capes, and Gitanillo received scattered applause. The second, Manolete's, showed even
less caste; he gave it a few derechazos in a dangerous terrain and
then, seeing that its will was ebbing rapidly, resorted to flashy and
meaningless adornos which dismayed the purists in the crowd. He
killed with a pinchazo and a forward estocada; "the bull," says
Señor Narbona, "deserved no better"; and the audience gently applauded.

Luis Miguel, eager to outdo the maestro, was lucky in a fine third
bull. He put in two pairs of sticks himself and brought off a neat
faena based on two series of naturals; though he killed less than
well, the crowd insisted that an ear be awarded. A slight misunderstanding followed, of a kind all too common in country rings; Luis

Miguel's head peon presented him with both ears and the tail. This overenthusiasm brought noisy protests, and Luis Miguel had to be content with a single trophy. With the fourth bull Gitanillo was uncertain and took no risks. Then came the fifth.

It was small and black, the number branded on its flank was 21, and its name was Islero. It was the one thousand and fourth bull of Manolete's career. During the preliminary rushes at the cape it halted menacingly, and disconcerted the banderilleros by a habit of turning suddenly in its own length. Standing in the callejón Camará noticed this and nudged Manolete:

"Manolo, I don't like him. Keep the cloth low and finish him off quickly."

The trumpet sounded, and Manolete set about coming to terms with the Miura. After a few punishment passes, low down with the right hand, he lifted the muleta for three slow passes en redondo. It was obvious by now that the bull favored its right horn. It was hooking toward the barrera all the time, and some of the crowd were getting restive. Icily proud, he calmed them with a sequence of his own majestic manoletinas. Guillermo, scared by this display of imprudence, hissed from the burladero: "Take it easy, maestro!"

Manolete did not hear. He went in to kill, but not safely, running out to the left of the horns, as most toreros would have done in the circumstances. He lined the bull up in the *suerte contraria*, with its left horn nearer to the barrera, so that his escape would be the perilous way, out to the middle of the ring.

It is said that Manolete's determination to outshine Luis Miguel was mainly responsible for the mighty volapié which followed. I prefer to think that he needed no spur to kill as he did. It was an estocada in slow motion. The bull stood twenty paces from the tunnel through which the toreros had entered the ring. Manolete drew back his shoulders and advanced inch by inch on the horns. Almost languidly, he pushed the sword home into the right place, up to the pommel. In that instant Islero raised his head, and stabbed his right horn, the bad one, into the upper part of Manolete's right thigh. He whirled up on the horn, spinning round on the point, which jabbed deeper into the wound with half a ton of Islero's weight behind it. He flew up and landed between the bull's forehoofs. David, Manolete's head peon, took the horns away with his cape. Guillermo was the first to run out to the stricken man's aid; after him Camará; and then the other peons, Cantimplas and El Sevillano. In their haste to reach the infirmary they carried Manolete, limp and etiolated, through the wrong door, and seconds passed before the bullring attendants showed them the right way.

Meanwhile Islero plodded over to the fence, and died. It was exactly forty-two minutes past six in the evening. "What happened afterward in the bullring in Linares," says Señor Narbona, "is no concern of history's."

The cheers pursued Manolete to the infirmary, but he was already insensible, and did not hear the last ovation of his life. When the doctors were completing their examination, David burst into the room with the ears and tail of Islero, which had been won so purely. Swarms of well-meaning onlookers filled the air with cigar smoke, and a jug of water had to be brought to moisten Manolete's lips. Blood was spurting from his leg in irregular gushes, and a transfusion was urgently required. The first volunteer was Juan Sánchez Calle, a police officer and close friend of the torero. While the operation was taking place, wooden chairs were being arranged in the bullring for the film show which had been announced for later in the evening, and a silent crowd gathered around Manolete's great blue car, which stood empty in the courtyard outside. A medical report was posted outside the infirmary. It said baldly that Manolete had been injured in the groin, and that the wound had taken three trajectories—inward, upward and downward: the result of the brief moment in which he had spun on the horn. The femoral artery was badly damaged, there was extensive hemorrhage and violent traumatic shock. "Outlook very grave." This was signed by Dr. Garrido and has been much commented on. Medical opinion now holds the view that Manolete was killed not by the wound itself but by the traumatic shock which it induced. Shock had unbalanced the vital triumvirate of brain, heart, and lungs by which we live; and his nervous system, already debilitated, could stand no further punishment. After a short conference, the doctors decided to summon the help of Jiménez Guinea, the Madrid bullring surgeon, who was spending the summer at El Escorial, more than two hundred miles to the north.

At eight o'clock Manolete regained consciousness. His peons were at his bedside, together with Camará, Gitanillo and Luis Miguel. He murmured to Cantimplas: "Ayee—but my groin hurts."

The peon mumbled a few words of comfort. Manolete turned toward Camará and asked: "Is it in a bad place?"

It was in the worst place, but no one spoke. He then asked for water, and Luis Miguel poured a little through his arid lips. At eight-thirty a second transfusion was performed. His resistance was still very low, but he revived enough to grip the hands of those around him, saying: "Move my leg a little. That's better. It was hurting me."

It was now agreed that he should be transferred to the municipal hospital in Linares. They carried him out of the infirmary on a stretcher. The crowd in the streets heard him utter two words. "Hurry!" he said: and again: "Hurry!" But the hospital of San

José was a good distance off, and twenty minutes passed before he was on the operating table. Meantime one of his peons telephoned the diestro's mother in San Sebastian.

"What has happened?" she said.

"Listen," he said, "Manolo has been caught in the leg. Yes, it's a cornada, but nothing special, nothing of any interest."

"Go on," said his mother.

"Well, he cut the ears and the tail. Pay no attention to the papers and the radio—you know what they are. All that stuff about arteries and so on! It isn't important. Don't alarm yourself."

Just after ten-thirty, one of his mother's friends, the impresario Pablo Martínez Elizondo, spoke to Camará by telephone from San Sebastian and heard the worst. As casually as he could, he suggested to the señora that she might like to be at her son's side. "Not that it's very serious, but I think he would be pleased to see you." At eleven they left together for Linares. "Of course if it was really bad," she said, "they would have taken him to Madrid."

By this time word of the goring had spread across the whole country; in Madrid, Seville, and Barcelona no one talked of anything else. At midnight a third blood transfusion was performed and Manolete was removed from the operating theater to a hospital bed. He asked for a cigarette, but could not smoke it: after three puffs it fell to the ground. He sighed, and said to Alvaro Domecq, the equestrian bullfighter, who had joined the group at the bedside:

"This is a bad feeling."

Professional pride revived for a moment, and he asked: "Did I kill the bull with that estocada?"

They told him he had killed it.

"And—didn't they give me an ear?"

Camará replied that they had given him both ears and the tail.

He smiled. A few minutes later, he shook his head and whispered: "How my mother will suffer!"

At 4 A.M. he began to grow terribly pale. He was able to recognize Domingo Ortega when the latter arrived, but could do no more than make a feeble gesture of apology. Shortly afterward Gitanillo, who had driven like a madman, drew up with Dr. Guinea in the blue car. Guinea examined the dying man and discussed the situation with Dr. Tamames, whom Luis Miguel had called in. They decided not to move him.

"Don Luis," said Manolete to Dr. Guinea, whom he knew well, "what can you do for me?"

Guinea told him to close his eyes and rest. To limit the circulation he then applied tighter bandages to both legs. Minutes passed, and Manolete said faintly: "I can't feel anything in my legs, doctor."

Guinea soothed him and again told him to rest. After a while he said: "I can't see you, Don Luis."

His eyes were open. Guinea said: "Close your eyes and don't worry. All is well."

There was no hope. A few minutes before five the hospital chaplain administered extreme unction. When this was done, Manolete called suddenly for his oldest peon: "David . . ."

His lips went on moving, but the words were lost. At seven minutes past five, as the sky was clearing over the town, a brief convulsion took place, but with it no great agony. Then Manolete's head slumped to the right, so that it faced a picture of the Virgin of the Macarena which stood by his bed. Dr. Tamames, who was taking his pulse, announced that he had given up his soul. Antonia, his mistress, who had been kept away from the deathbed for fear of the effect her appearance might have on him, was now admitted, to weep over his body.

In the hospital chapel the first mass was celebrated in his memory. A little after ten o'clock his remains were taken in an ambulance to Córdoba, where they are now buried.

Deaths such as this have their echoes. All of Spain mourned Manolete, and with some members of his profession his mischance became a morbid preoccupation. On September 14, just over two weeks after the disaster of Linares, the Mexican bullfighter José González López, known as Carnicerito de Mexico, was gored in the Portuguese bullring of Vila Vicosa. He was forty years old, competent with the cape and muleta and an acknowledged maestro with the banderillas. His second bull, a difficult manso, came treacherously to the faena, and, after submitting to two valiant statuary passes, caught Carnicerito high up in the right leg, severing the femoral artery. As he was being carried to the hospital, half a mile away, he said:

"Don't leave me. Take care of me. My cornada is like Manolete's."

He was convinced that he had been chosen to relive Manolete's anguish, and nothing would dislodge the idea from his mind. He mouthed Manolete's words: "I can't feel anything in my legs, doctor. . . ."

And later: "I can't see you, Don Luis. . . ."

At half past six next morning he called for extreme unction. Two hours later he began to sink, and Conchita Cintrón, the *rejoneadora*, bent over to decipher his last words.

"Watch me," he said, "I am dying like Manolete."